ck Vandome

Windows 10

in easy steps

3rd edition
Updated for the Windows 10 Creators Update

In easy steps is an imprint of In Easy Steps Limited
16 Hamilton Terrace · Holly Walk · Leamington Spa
Warwickshire · United Kingdom · CV32 4LY
www.ineasysteps.com

Third Edition

Notice of Liability
Every effort has been made to ensure that this book contains accurate
and current information. However, In Easy Steps Limited and the
author shall not be liable for any loss or damage suffered by readers
as a result of any information contained herein.

Trademarks
Microsoft® and Windows® are registered trademarks of Microsoft
Corporation. All other trademarks are acknowledged as belonging to
their respective companies.

In Easy Steps Limited supports The Forest Stewardship Council (FSC),
the leading international forest certification organization. All our titles
that are printed on Greenpeace approved FSC certified paper carry the
FSC logo.

MIX
Paper from
responsible sources
FSC® C020837

Printed and bound in the United Kingdom

ISBN 978-1-84078-789-4

Contents

Standard Controls 91

Customizing Windows 107

File Explorer 121

1 Introducing Windows 10

This chapter explains what Windows is, and shows how to get started with the operating system, including the changes in Windows 10 Creators Update and its interface, keyboard shortcuts, creating a Microsoft Account and signing in.

What is Windows?

Windows is an operating system for PCs (personal computers), laptops and tablets. The operating system is the software that organizes and controls all of the components (hardware and software) in your computer.

The first operating system from Microsoft was known as MS-DOS (Microsoft Disk Operating System). This was a non-graphical, line-oriented, command-driven operating system, able to run only one application at a time. The original Windows system was an interface manager that ran on top of the MS-DOS system, providing a graphical user interface (GUI) and using clever processor and memory management to allow it to run more than one application or function at a time.

The basic element of Windows was its "windowing" capability. A window (with a lower-case w) is a rectangular area used to display information or to run a program or app. Several windows can be opened at the same time so that you can work with multiple applications. This provided a dramatic increase in productivity, in comparison with the original MS-DOS.

Microsoft released four versions of this interface management Windows, with numerous intermediate versions, including:

- 1985 – Windows 1.0 ● 1987 – Windows 2.0, 2.1 & 2.11
- 1990 – Windows 3.0, 3.1, 3.11 (Windows for Workgroups)
- 1995 – Windows 95 ● 1998 – Windows 98, 98 SE
- 2000 – Windows Me (Millennium Edition)

The next version, Windows XP, was a full operating system in its own right. This was followed by Windows Vista and then Windows 7, 8, 8.1 and 10 (there was no Windows 9).

- 2001 – Windows XP (eXPerience) Home and Professional
- 2007 – Windows Vista Home, Home Premium, Ultimate etc.
- 2009 – Windows 7 Starter, Home Premium, Ultimate etc.
- 2012 – Windows 8 Starter, Pro, Enterprise and RT
- 2013 – Windows 8.1 Starter, Pro, Enterprise and RT
- 2015 – Windows 10 Home, Pro, Enterprise and Education
- 2016 – Windows 10 Anniversary Update

The New icon pictured above indicates a new or enhanced feature introduced with the Windows 10 Creators Update.

About Windows 10

The latest version of Windows was released in April 2017:

- 2017 – Windows 10 Creators Update, which can be used to upgrade any existing version of Windows 10.

All major computer operating systems (OS) undergo regular upgrades and new versions. Sometimes these are a significant visual overhaul, while others concentrate more on the behind-the-scenes aspect of the OS. In terms of Microsoft Windows, Windows 8 was one of the most radical updates to the User Interface (UI), and introduced a number of new features for both desktop and mobile versions of Windows. However, it was not met with universal approval, as it was perceived that it was two separate operating systems (desktop and mobile) bolted together, and not satisfying either environment completely.

With Windows 10, a lot of the problems with Windows 8 were addressed: the familiar Start menu was reinstated to return to a UI similar to earlier versions of Windows; there was a greater consolidation between desktop and mobile devices running Windows 10; and the operation of apps was standardized so that it is similar for the new Windows apps as well as the more traditional ones. In a sense, this was a case of going back one step in order to go forwards two steps, and Windows 10 has succeeded in creating a familiar environment, coupled with a range of innovative and useful features.

Windows 10 Creators Update

The intention for Windows 10 has always been to produce incremental updates, rather than waiting a period of time for the next major update. This is the reason why it is unlikely that there will be a Windows 11; instead, there will be regular online updates to Windows 10. The Windows 10 Creators Update marks the second anniversary of the release of the software. It contains a number of improvements and refinements but, in keeping with the Windows 10 ethos, it is an incremental update rather than a major new operating system, although it contains a comprehensive range of new features. The Creators Update is delivered online through the Windows Update function in the Settings app. A registered version of Windows 10 has to be installed in order for the Creators Update to be downloaded (or a license can be bought when downloading the Creators Update). Some of the new features in the update are detailed on the next two pages.

If you are upgrading to Windows 10 from Windows 7, 8 or 8.1, you will be able to keep all of your settings, files and apps.

The functionality of the Creators Update is generally the same as for the original Windows 10, and it will, in general, be referred to as Windows 10 throughout the book.

Microsoft has also announced a version of Windows 10 named Windows 10 S. This is designed to only use apps from the Windows Store, and is aimed at the education market and users who prefer to remove the risk of using non-Windows Store apps.

About Creators Update

Although the Creators Update is still under the Windows 10 banner, there is a range of significant additions and enhancements from the earlier versions of the operating system. Some of these include:

These features are new or updated in the Windows 10 Creators Update.

- **Enhanced Settings**. The Settings app has been updated to include more options, and also more of the items in the Windows Control Panel have been migrated to the Settings app so that they can be found in one place. One example of this is the Themes option, which can be used to apply personalized themes across the whole of Windows 10.

- **Gaming Settings**. There is a new Settings category for Gaming, and there is also a new Game Bar that is a virtual games controller, which can be activated when playing games with Windows 10 Creators Update.

- **Start menu folders**. The Start menu has been enhanced, with the option of creating folders on the Start menu so that several items can be stored and accessed within one menu tile.

- **Cortana commands**. Cortana, the Windows 10 personal digital assistant has new voice commands for turning off, sleeping or restarting a PC, and also a greater range of apps now support Cortana.

- **Edge tabs**. The Microsoft Edge web browser has enhanced tabs functions, whereby they can be grouped together and also previewed by moving the cursor over a tab.

- **Share menu**. The Share menu has been redesigned to display apps with which certain items can be shared, and this is available from the Share button in a range of apps.

3D in Creators Update

3D features prominently in the Windows 10 Creators Update, with a new app, Paint 3D, for creating your own 3D pictures. It also supplies the Remix 3D service, which is a Microsoft website where 3D objects from other users can be viewed and downloaded for use in your own projects.

Other 3D enhancements include being able to upload and view 3D images in the Edge web browser, and 3D models can be used in PowerPoint for transitions between slides.

Items created in Paint 3D can be used in a Mixed Reality environment using the HoloLens headset.

Mixed Reality

Developing the 3D theme further, the Windows 10 Creators Update also includes a number of Mixed Reality (MR) features. Mixed Reality is the combining of the real and virtual worlds to create a unique user experience. This is usually done through the use of a Mixed Reality headset – the Microsoft one is called HoloLens. When this is worn, 3D objects and holograms can be viewed within the user's actual environment, i.e. you can view an array of objects while still viewing the physical elements of a room in your home. However, the HoloLens is expensive, and Microsoft is addressing this by developing a range of Mixed Reality headsets with other manufacturers. Although Mixed Reality is still in its relative infancy in terms of mainstream adoption, it is something that is going to develop greatly in the coming years.

The Windows 10 Creators Update includes a **Mixed Reality Portal** app that gives a useful overview of using Mixed Reality with the Windows 10 Creators Update.

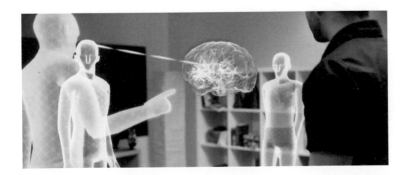

Mixed Reality requires PCs with higher processor and graphics card capabilities than for general computing.

11

Windows 10 Interface

Windows 8 was one of the most significant changes to the Windows operating system since Windows 95 helped redefine the way that we look at personal computers. It aimed to bring the desktop and mobile computing environments together, principally with the brightly colored Start screen and Charms bar. However, this proved to be awkward for a lot of users, with Windows 8 not fully meeting the needs of the device being used.

The original Windows 10 interface was redesigned so that it looked as similar as possible, regardless of whether it is being used on a desktop computer with a mouse and keyboard, or on a mobile or touchscreen device (and most of the underlying functionality is still the same). The first major upgrade of Windows 10, the Anniversary Update, saw one significant change, in that the operating system recognized the type of device being used and amended the interface accordingly. The Windows 10 Creators Update keeps the same interface as the Anniversary Update, while adding some visual updates, such as an option for minimizing the alphabetic list of all apps on the Start menu, and some internal improvements to ensure that Windows 10 runs more efficiently.

As with the original Windows 10, the Creators Update looks more familiar to users of pre-Windows 8 versions of Windows. It opens at the Desktop, where shortcuts to items can be placed, and the Taskbar is at the bottom of the screen.

Don't forget

The main recommended specifications for PCs and laptops running the Windows 10 Creators Update are: 1GHz processor; 1GB RAM (32-bit Windows) or 2GB RAM (64-bit Windows); and 16GB (32-bit Windows) or 20GB (64-bit Windows) of free disk space for installation.

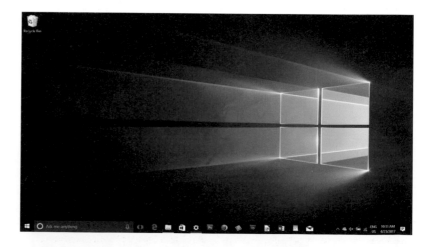

...cont'd

Start menu

The Start menu was reinstated in the original version of Windows 10, although it has been redesigned so that it also includes a range of colored tiles, which can be pinned to the Start menu and are used to access the most commonly used or favorite apps. The left-hand side of the Start menu contains links to some of your most frequently used functions, such as the Power button, the Settings app, the File Explorer, the Most used apps and the alphabetic list of all of the apps on the PC.

The Settings app can be used to customize the Start menu (**Settings > Personalization > Start**). See page 45 for more details.

Windows 10 for touchscreen

The Windows 10 version that is optimized for touchscreen use is designed for using with a tablet (such as the Microsoft Surface Pro), where all of the screen navigation can be done by

tapping, swiping and pinching on the screen. These features can also be used on touchscreen desktops and laptops that have this functionality (see page 16 for details). Some tablets also have a detachable keyboard that can be used with standard controls.

Obtaining Windows 10

Windows 10 is a slight departure by Microsoft in that it is promoted as an online service, rather than just a standalone operating system. This means that, by default, Windows 10 is obtained and downloaded online, with subsequent updates and upgrades provided on a regular basis.

The original version of Windows 10 was a free upgrade if it was downloaded and installed by July 2016. Windows 10 can now be bought from the Microsoft website, or through software retailers. A registered version of Windows 10 has to been installed before the free Creators Update can be downloaded, unless a PC is running Windows 7 or 8, in which case it can be upgraded to the Creators Update if a license is bought.

The three main options for obtaining the Windows 10 Creators Update are:

For more information about the Settings app, see pages 40-53.

- **Use Windows Update** – Replace an older version of Windows 10, retaining the installed applications and settings. This can be done through the **Settings** app (select **Update & security > Windows Update** and click on the **Check for updates** button).

- **Microsoft website** – visit the software download page on the Microsoft website (**microsoft.com/en-us/software-download/windows10**) to use the **Update Assistant** to download the Windows 10 Creators Update.

- **Pre-install** – Buy a new PC or laptop with the Windows 10 Creators Update already installed.

Some of the steps that the installation will go through are:

Applying Privacy settings during the setup process is a new feature in the Windows 10 Creators Update.

- **Personalize**. These are settings that will be applied to your version of Windows 10. These settings can also be selected within the Settings app once Windows 10 has been installed.

- **Settings**. You can choose to have express settings applied, or customize them.

- **Microsoft Account**. You can set up a Microsoft Account during installation, or once you have started Windows 10.

- **Privacy**. Certain privacy settings can be applied during the setup process for the Windows 10 Creators Update.

Keyboard Shortcuts

As you become more confident using Windows 10 you may want to access certain items more quickly. There is a range of keyboard shortcuts that can be used to access some of the items you use most frequently.

The majority of the shortcuts are accessed together with the WinKey (Windows key). on the keyboard. To use the keyboard shortcuts press:

- **WinKey** to access the Start menu at any time.

- **WinKey** + **L** to lock the computer and display the Lock screen.

- **WinKey** + **I** to access the Settings app.

- **WinKey** + **K** to connect new devices.

- **WinKey** + **Q** to access the personal digital assistant voice function, Cortana.

- **WinKey** + **D** to access the Desktop.

- **WinKey** + **M** to access the Desktop with the active window minimized.

- **WinKey** + **E** to access File Explorer, displaying the Quick access section.

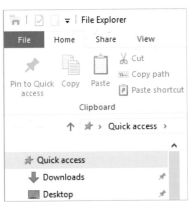

- **WinKey** + **T** to display the thumbnails on the Desktop Taskbar.

- **WinKey** + **U** to access the Ease of Access Center.

- **WinKey** + **X** to access the Power User menu, which gives you quick access to items including the Desktop and File Explorer.

- **Alt** + **F4** to close a Windows 10 app.

- **Ctrl** + **Shift** + **Esc** to access the Task Manager.

Windows 10 for Touch

One of the aims of Windows 10 is to make the operating system more familiar again to users with a keyboard and mouse. This has been done by reverting back to a more traditional look and feel than that of Windows 8 and 8.1. For touchscreen devices such as tablets, laptops with precision touchpads, and phones, the same overall operation of Windows 10 has been maintained so that users can feel comfortable with the operating system regardless of the device on which they are using it.

Continuum

Continuum refers to the function of Windows 10 where you can start something on one Windows 10 device and then continue working on it on another. For instance, you could start a letter in Word on a desktop computer, save it, and then pick up where you left off on the Microsoft tablet, Surface. Continuum works between desktop computers, laptops, tablets and Windows phones.

Using touch

Touchscreen devices and those with precision touchpads can be used with Windows 10 to navigate through a number of gestures, swipes and taps on the screen or touchpad. The range of these gestures has been consolidated from Windows 8 and 8.1, since these included a number of options for accessing the Charms that are no longer available with Windows 10. Some of the gestures that can be used with touchscreen or touchpad devices using Windows 10 are:

- Swipe inwards from the right-hand edge to access the Notification panel (Action Center).

- Swipe inwards from the left-hand edge to access the Task View for currently open apps.

- In an open Windows 10 app, swipe downwards from the top of the screen to access the app's toolbar.

- In an open Windows 10 app, use a long swipe downwards from the top of the screen to close the app.

- Swipe upwards from the bottom of the screen to access the Taskbar (when an app is at full screen).

- Tap with three fingers on a touchpad to bring up the personal digital assistant, Cortana.

The Windows 10 Creators Update has enhanced Windows Ink, which enables users of a touchscreen device to jot down notes, make sketches and launch some apps, using a compatible pen.

Aside from the gestures used on a touchscreen device, much of the operation of Windows 10 has been consolidated between computers with a mouse and keyboard, and mobile devices.

Control Panel and Settings

In previous versions of Windows, the Control Panel played an important role in applying settings for a number of different functions. Because of this, it could be accessed in several different ways. However, in the Windows 10 Creators Update, more of the Control Panel functionality has been moved to the Settings app, and there are fewer methods for accessing the Control Panel. Despite this, it can still be used to access a variety of settings:

1 Click on the **Start** button to access the **Start** menu for accessing apps

2 Click on the **Windows System** button

Windows System

3 Click on the **Control Panel** button

Control Panel

4 Click on the **Control Panel** categories to view the content within them

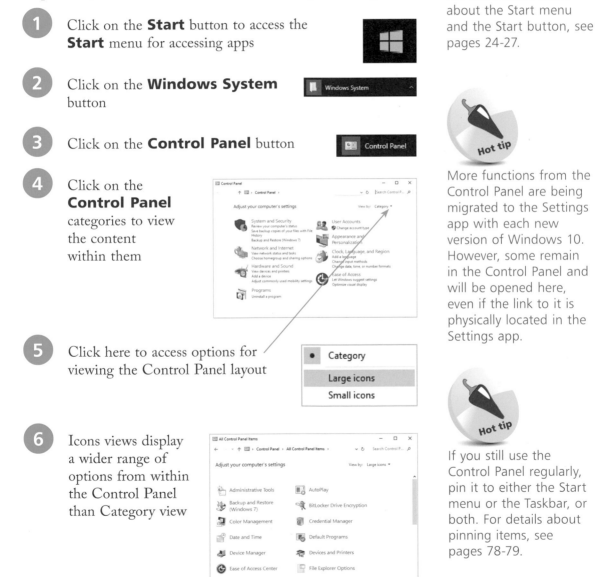

5 Click here to access options for viewing the Control Panel layout

- Category
- Large icons
- Small icons

6 Icons views display a wider range of options from within the Control Panel than Category view

Don't forget

For more information about the Start menu and the Start button, see pages 24-27.

Hot tip

More functions from the Control Panel are being migrated to the Settings app with each new version of Windows 10. However, some remain in the Control Panel and will be opened here, even if the link to it is physically located in the Settings app.

17

Hot tip

If you still use the Control Panel regularly, pin it to either the Start menu or the Taskbar, or both. For details about pinning items, see pages 78-79.

Using a Microsoft Account

We live in a world of ever-increasing computer connectivity, where users expect to be able to access their content wherever they are and share it with their friends and family in a variety of ways, whether it is by email, messaging or photo sharing. This is known as Cloud computing, with content being stored on online servers, from where it can be accessed by authorized users.

In Windows 10, this type of connectivity is achieved with a Microsoft Account. This is a registration system (which can be set up with most email addresses and a password) that provides access to a number of services via the Windows 10 apps. These include:

- **Mail**. This is the Windows 10 email app that can be used to access and manage your different email accounts.

- **Skype**. This is the text messaging and video chatting app.

- **People**. This is the address book app.

- **Calendar**. This is the calendar and organizer app.

- **Windows Store**. This is the online store for previewing and downloading additional apps.

- **OneDrive**. This is the online backup and sharing service.

Creating a Microsoft Account

It is free to create a Microsoft Account. This can be done with an email address and, together with a password, provides a unique identifier for logging into your Microsoft Account and the related apps. There are several ways in which you can create and set up a Microsoft Account:

- During the initial setup process when you install Windows 10. You will be asked if you want to create a Microsoft Account at this point. If you do not, you can always do so at a later time.

- When you first open an app that requires access to a Microsoft Account. When you do this you will be prompted to create a new account.

- From the **Accounts** section of the **Settings** app (see page 47).

Beware

Without a Microsoft Account you will not be able to access the full functionality of the apps listed here.

...cont'd

Whichever way you use to create a Microsoft Account, the process is similar:

1 When you are first prompted to sign in with a Microsoft Account you can enter your account details, if you have one, or

> **Make it yours**
> Your Microsoft account opens a world of benefits. Learn more
>
> [Email, phone, or Skype name]
> [Password]
> Forgot my password
>
> No account? Create one!
>
> Microsoft privacy statement
> [Sign in]

2 Click on the **No account? Create one!** link

> No account? Create one!

3 Enter your name, an email address and a password for your Microsoft Account

> **Let's create your account**
> Windows, Office, Outlook.com, OneDrive, Skype, Xbox. They're all better and more personal when you sign in with your Microsoft account.* Learn more
>
> [nickvandome@gmail.com   ×]
> Get a new email address
> [Password]
> [United Kingdom   ∨]
>
> *If you already use a Microsoft service, go Back to sign in with that account.
> [Next] [Back]

Hot tip

Microsoft Account details can also be used as your sign-in for Windows 10 (see pages 20-21).

19

4 Click on the **Next** button to move through the registration process

> [Next]

5 Enter your password again to confirm your account

6 Click on the **Finish** button in the final window to complete setting up your Microsoft Account

> **Sign in to this device using your Microsoft account**
> From here on out, you'll unlock this device using either the password for your Microsoft account or, if you've set one up, your PIN. That way, you can get help from Cortana, you can find your device if you lose it, and your settings will automatically sync.
>
> To make sure it's really you, we'll need your current Windows password one last time. Next time you sign into Windows you'll use your Microsoft account password.
>
> If you don't have a Windows password, just leave the box blank and select Next.
>
> Current Windows password
> [|]
>
> [Next]

Sign-in Options

Each time you start up your computer you will need to sign in. This is a security feature so that no-one can gain unauthorized access to your account on your PC. The sign-in process starts with the Lock screen and then you have to enter your sign-in password.

Don't forget

For details about personalizing the Lock screen see page 45.

1 When you start your PC the Lock screen will be showing. This is linked to the sign-in screen

11:27
Friday, April 28

Hot tip

You can lock your PC at any time by pressing **WinKey** + **L**.

2 Click on the **Lock screen**, or press any key to move to the sign-in screen. Enter your password and press **Enter**, or click on this arrow

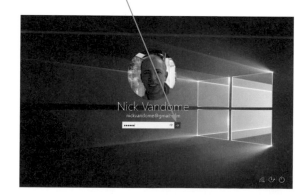

Nick Vandome
nickvandome@gmail.com

Don't forget

You will get an error message if you enter the wrong password or if you simply mis-key and cause an incorrect character to be added.

3 On the sign-in screen, click on this button to select Ease of Access options

4 On the sign-in screen, click on this button to select Power off options including Shut down and Restart

5 If there are other users with an account on the same PC, their names will be displayed here

You can sign in with a Local account or a Microsoft Account. If you sign in with the latter, you will have access to the related services, such as Mail and People. Also, you will be able to sync your settings and use them on another computer when you log in with your account.

6 Click on another user to access their own sign-in screen

Sign-in settings
Settings for how you sign in can be accessed from the Accounts section in the Settings app:

1 Access the **Settings** app and click on the **Accounts** button

For details about using the Settings app see pages 40-53.

2 Under **Sign-in options**, select options to change your password, create a picture password or create a PIN instead of a password

3 If you want to create a picture password you must have a touchscreen device. Select a picture and draw a pattern to use as your sign-in

Windows Hello is a function that uses biometric authentication for signing in to Windows 10. This is either done by scanning your face, or with a fingerprint reader. However, specialist hardware is required and this is not available on many devices at present.

32-Bit versus 64-Bit

When installing Windows 10, you may need to decide between the 32-bit and the 64-bit versions of the operating system. When the Windows 10 Creators Update is downloaded, it should match the version that is already installed, in terms of 32- or 64-bit.

The 32-bit or 64-bit nomenclature refers to the memory address length which the processor can reference. This dictates the maximum amount of memory, which is 4GB for 32-bit mode (or more accurately 3.4GB, since some memory needs to be allocated for other purposes). For 64-bit mode, the maximum may be much higher, and as well as more memory, 64-bit mode will also be faster; typically about 10%.

However, you need applications that are specifically optimized for 64-bit processing to take advantage of the speed improvements and memory increase. Many games, for example, include the necessary enhancements.

Remember that choosing a 64-bit system means that you can no longer run 16-bit applications. This is only a problem if you use very old software (from the Windows 3.1 days).

More importantly, existing 32-bit drivers for your devices will not operate in 64-bit mode, so you will have to locate 64-bit versions of the drivers. You may have problems with some devices, particularly the older ones.

You may also find that running 32-bit applications in a 64-bit operating system might actually be slower, due to the additional overheads imposed by conversion between the address systems.

If you have a 64-bit capable computer but use older hardware or 32-bit applications, you might do better to stay with the 32-bit version of Windows 10. With the latest hardware and drivers, and applications that are 64-bit optimized, for especially demanding applications such as video editing or image packages, the switch to 64-bit and higher memory would offer significant improvements.

It will not be long before 64-bit computing becomes the standard, and 32-bit operation becomes an optional extra, but for the present there are still large numbers of 32-bit applications.

Hot tip

To check whether your version of Windows 10 is 32-bit or 64-bit, click on the **Settings** app. Select **System** > **About** and look under the **System type** heading.

2 Getting Started

The Windows 10 Creators Update improves further upon the version of the Windows operating system that was a considerable step forward after the Windows 8 version. This chapter looks at some of the main features of the Windows 10 Creators Update, focusing on the Start menu and using the Desktop and the Taskbar. It also covers the personal digital assistant, Cortana, for voice searching over your computer for a range of items, and setting reminders.

The Start Button

The Start button has been a significant part of Windows computing for numerous versions of the operating system. There was a change in the traditional use of the Start button with the introduction of Windows 8, but this was met with widespread disapproval and the Start button has since been reinstated. In the Windows 10 Creators Update, the Start button works in a similar way to most early version of Windows, with some enhancements.

Using the Start button

The Start button provides access to the apps on your Windows 10 PC and also to the enhanced Start menu:

 Click on the **Start** button in the bottom left-hand corner of the screen

 The **Start** menu is displayed

The items on the Start menu can be customized from the **Personalization** > **Start** section of the Settings app.

3 The left-hand side of the Start menu contains links to frequently used apps, a list of quick links to items such as the Power button, and an alphabetic list of all of the apps on the computer

Click on the **Power** button on the Start menu to access options for Sleep, Shut down or Restart.

4 The right-hand side of the Start menu is where apps can be pinned so that they are always available. These are displayed as a collection of large, colored tiles

 Other items can also be accessed from the Start button by right-clicking on it

Power User menu

In addition to accessing the Start menu, the Start button also provides
access to the Power User menu, which can be accessed as follows:

 Right-click on the
Start button to view
the Power User menu

2 Click on the relevant
buttons to view items
including the **Desktop**
and other popular
locations such as the
File Explorer

Apps and Features

Mobility Center

Power Options

Event Viewer

System

Device Manager

Network Connections

Disk Management

Computer Management

Windows PowerShell

Windows PowerShell (Admin)

Task Manager

Settings

File Explorer

Search

Run

Shut down or sign out   >

Desktop

> **Don't forget**
>
> The Start button Power
> User menu in Step 1 has
> a number of options
> for accessing system
> functions, such as
> Command Prompt and
> Disk Management.

25

Task Manager

Settings

File Explorer

Search

Run

Shut down or sign out   >

Desktop

3 **Shut down or sign out** options are also available
from the **Start** button (see page 35)

The Start Menu

The Start menu in Windows 10 is where you can access areas within your computer, perform certain functions, and also access apps from a variety of locations. Some of the default items on the Start menu can be customized to a certain extent (see pages 28-29) and there is considerable functionality here:

1 Your most frequently used apps are displayed here. Click on one to open it (these items will change as you use different apps)

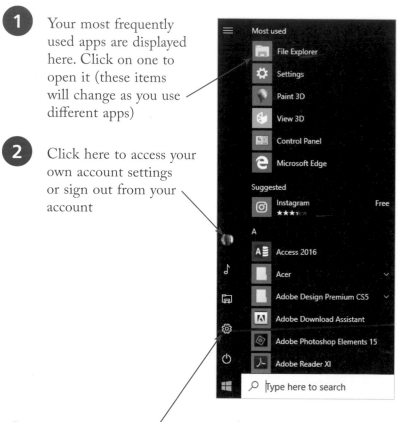

2 Click here to access your own account settings or sign out from your account

3 Click here to access items including the **File Explorer**, your **Documents** library within File Explorer and the Windows 10 **Settings**

4 Click on the **Power** button for options to **Sleep** your computer, **Shut down** or **Restart**

5 Use the scroll bar at the right-hand side to move through the list of apps

Click on a letter at the top of a section of apps to view an alphabetic grid. Click on a letter to move to that section.

6 If there is a down-pointing arrow next to an app, this means that there are additional items that can be accessed. Click on the arrow to view these

Customizing the Start Menu

Windows 10 is very adaptable and can be customized in several ways, so that it works best for you. This includes the Start menu which can be set to behave in certain ways and have specific items added to it. To do this:

1 Open the **Settings** app and click on the **Personalization** button

2 Click on the **Start** button

Beware

Full screen mode is designed more for tablets, and if you use it, the Start menu will occupy the whole screen.

3 Under **Preview**, select whether to show suggestions for apps on the Start menu, show most used apps or recently used apps on the Start menu or show the Start menu full screen (scroll up the page to view this, below the **Occasionally show suggestions in Start** button)

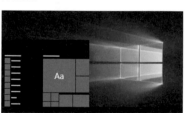

4 Click on the **Choose which folders appear on Start** button to select the items that appear on the Start menu

| Choose which folders appear on Start |

5 Drag the buttons **On** for the items you want to appear on the Start menu, i.e. the File Explorer, the Settings app, the Documents library, and the Music app

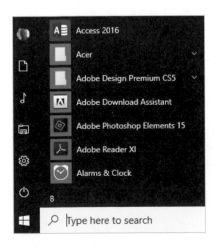

6 The items selected in Step 5 appear on the Start menu, above the Power button

If you find that you do not use some items very much once they have been added to the Start menu, they can be removed by dragging their buttons to **Off** in Step 5.

29

Working with Groups

By default, the apps on the Start menu are arranged in groups, such as Everyday apps. However, apps can be arranged into other groups, and new ones can also be created, by dragging apps between groups. To do this:

 Click and hold on a tile and drag it into another group to place it here. If there is no space, the other apps will move to accommodate the new one

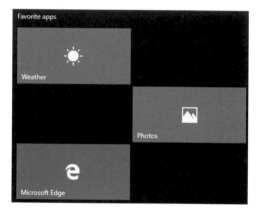

 Drag the tile into an empty space to create a new group

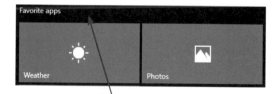

3 Click and drag on the title bar of a group to move the whole group

Naming groups

In their initial state, groups on the Start menu are either not named, or they have a default name, but it is possible to give them all their own individual names or titles. To do this:

1 Move the cursor over the top of a group and click on the current name or on this button at the right-hand side

Everyday apps ═

2 Double-click on the current name

Everyday apps

3 Enter a new name for the group

My best apps|

4 The name is applied at the top of the group

Hot tip

Group names can be edited using the same process as when creating them in the first place.

Resizing Tiles

As well as rearranging tiles, their sizes can also be edited on the Start menu. Depending on the specific Windows app, there may be up to four options for resizing tiles in Windows 10: wide, large, medium and small, with the initial selection made for you:

 Right-click on a tile to select it, and click on the **Resize** button from the context menu which appears

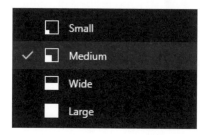

 The current size of the tile is shown with a tick next to it

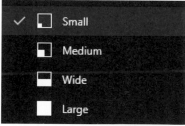

 Click on another option to resize the tile

 If the size is made smaller, the tile is reduced in size and a gap appears around it (unless there is another tile small enough to fill the space next to it)

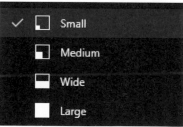

5 For a wide tile, there will be options for making it **Large**, **Medium** or **Small**

Hot tip

The **Large** size is a good option for a tile that can then be used as a Live Tile, to display its contents or real-time information (see page 85).

Creating Folders

Tiles can be pinned to the Start menu (see page 78), which means that over time it can begin to appear a bit cluttered, with dozens of tiles competing for space. To help organize the Start menu, there is an option for creating folders, so that similar apps can be grouped together within the one tile. To do this:

Folders on the Start menu is a new feature in the Windows 10 Creators Update.

 1 Drag one tile over another to create the group. Ideally the tiles should be for similar types of apps, e.g. for entertainment

2 The two apps are displayed in the newly-created folder

3 Click on a folder to view its contents. Click on this button to minimize the folder again

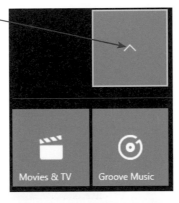

4 To remove an app from a folder, open the folder and drag the app out of the folder and back onto the Start menu

The Desktop can also be accessed by pressing **WinKey + D** or by right-clicking on the Start button and selecting **Desktop**.

Don't forget

If an app has two or more windows open, each of them will be displayed when you move the cursor over the app's icon on the Taskbar.

34

Don't forget

You can customize the Notification area by right-clicking on an empty area on the Taskbar, clicking on **Taskbar settings** and then clicking **Select which icons appear on the taskbar** underneath the Notification area sub-heading.

The Desktop and Taskbar

After the use of the Start Screen in Windows 8 and 8.1, the Desktop is once again an integral part of Windows, and when you boot up Windows 10 it opens at the Desktop. This also displays the Taskbar at the bottom of the screen:

Shortcut icons   Search box/Cortana   Desktop background

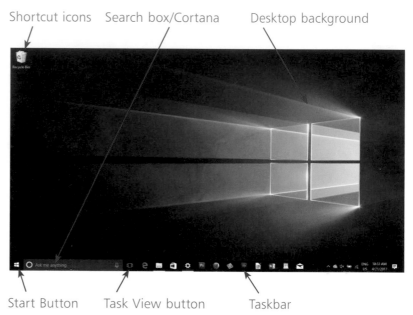

Start Button   Task View button   Taskbar

 Move the cursor over items on the Taskbar to see open windows for that item. Click on a window to make that the active one

 The Notification area at the right-hand side of the Taskbar has speaker, network and other system tools. Click on one to see more information about that item

Shutting Down

Options for shutting down Windows have been amended with some versions of the operating system. In the Windows 10 Creators Update, this functionality can be accessed from the Start menu.

Shutting down from the Start menu

1 Click on the **Start** button

2 Right-click on the **Power** button

3 Click on either the **Sleep**, **Shut down** or **Restart** buttons; or

For some updates to Windows, you will need to restart your computer for them to take effect.

4 Right-click on the **Start** button and select either **Sign out**, **Sleep**, **Shut down** or **Restart** from the **Shut down or sign out** option

Task View

A useful feature in Windows 10 is the Task View option. This is located on the Taskbar and can be used to view all open apps and also add new desktops. To use Task View:

1 Click on this button on the Taskbar

2 To show or hide the Task View button, right-click on the button and check On or Off the **Show Task View button** option

Apps can only be open on one desktop at a time. So, if an app is open on one desktop and you try to open it on another, you will be taken to the desktop with the already open app. For adding additional desktops, see the next page.

3 The Task View displays minimized versions of the currently open apps and windows

4 As more windows are opened, the format is arranged accordingly

Although the shortcuts and background are the same for each Desktop, the Taskbar will change depending on the open apps.

5 If an app has more than one window open, e.g. File Explorer, each window is displayed within Task View

6 Click on a window in Task View to make it the active window

Adding Desktops

Another function within Task View is for creating additional desktops. This can be useful if you want to separate different categories of tasks on your computer. For instance, you may want to keep your open entertainment apps on a different desktop to your productivity ones. To create additional desktops:

 Click on the **Task View** button on the Taskbar

 The current desktop is displayed with the open windows

 Click on the **New desktop** button

The new desktop is displayed at the bottom of the Task View window

Click on the new desktop to access it. Each desktop has the same background and shortcuts

Open apps on the new desktop. These will be separate from the apps on any other desktop

If you add too many desktops it may become confusing in terms of the content on each one.

The default names of different desktops cannot be changed, i.e. they are Desktop 1, Desktop 2, etc.

To delete a desktop, click on the Task View button and click on the cross that appears when you hover your mouse over the desktop you want to remove.

Click on the **Task View** button to move between desktops.

Notifications

There are some enhancements in the Action Center's Notifications panel in the Windows 10 Creators Update. Similar notifications can now be grouped together; the Quick Actions buttons have been enhanced; and some notifications (such as those for apps that are downloading) have progress bars to indicate how far through the operation they are.

Click on a notification to open it and view its full contents.

Notifications for certain apps also appear on screen for a short period of time in a small banner, to alert you to the fact that there is a new notification.

In the modern digital world there is an increasing desire to keep updated about what is happening in our online world. With Windows 10, the Action Center (which contains the Notifications panel) can be used to display information from a variety of sources, so that you never miss an update or a notification from one of your apps. To view your notifications:

 Click on the **Action Center** button on the Taskbar

 New notifications appear at the top of the panel. For selecting what appears, see the next page

 Quick action buttons appear at the bottom of the panel. Click on an item to activate or deactivate it (when a button is blue, the item is active)

Settings for notifications

To change settings for the Action Center:

1 Click on the **Settings** app and access **System > Notifications & actions**

System

☐ Display

☐ Notifications & actions

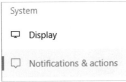

Hot tip

If notification icons are added to the Taskbar, their options can be selected by right-clicking on them.

2 Under the **Quick actions** heading, click on the items and drag them into a new position to change where they appear in the Notifications panel

Quick actions

Press and hold (or select) quick actions, then drag to rearrange them. These quick actions appear in action center.

Tablet mode | Network | Note | All settings
Airplane mode | Location | Quiet hours | Brightness
Bluetooth | VPN | Battery saver | Project
Connect | Mobile hotspot | Night light

Add or remove quick actions

3 Click on the **Add or remove quick actions** link to turn **On** or **Off** the default items on the Taskbar

⚙ Add or remove quick actions

⚙ All settings — On
📶 Network — On
⬚ Connect — Off
🗗 Project — On
◊ Battery saver — On

Hot tip

Notifications can also be shown on the Lock screen by dragging the **Show notifications on the lock screen** button to **On** in the **Notifications & actions** settings.

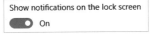

Show notifications on the lock screen
◯ On

4 Under the **Get notifications from these senders** heading, drag the buttons **On** or **Off** to specify the items that appear in the Action Center. For instance, if the **Mail** button is **On**, you will be notified whenever you receive a new email

Get notifications from these senders

Select a sender to see more settings. Some senders might also have their own notification settings. If so, open the sender to change them.

AutoPlay
On: Banners, Sounds — On

Battery saver
On: Banners, Sounds — On

Calendar
On: Banners, Sounds — On

Settings

Accessing Settings

The Settings in Windows 10 provide options for how you set up your computer and how it operates. There are 11 main categories of Settings, each of which have a number of sub-categories. The Settings app can be accessed in a number of ways:

 Click on the **Start** button

 Click on the **Settings** button on the Start menu or the **Settings** tile on the Start menu, or

 Click on the **Action Center** button on the Taskbar

 Click on the **All settings** button; or

 Enter **Settings** into the **Search** box and click on the **Settings** button

 In the **Settings** app, click on one of the main categories to view the options within that category

Add the **Settings** app to the Taskbar for quick access. To do this, access it from the Start menu, right-click on it and click on **More** > **Pin to taskbar**.

System Settings

The System Settings provide numerous options to specify how your computer looks and operates. They include:

- **Display**. This contains options for changing the size of items on the screen, the orientation of the screen, and options for adjusting the screen brightness, either manually or automatically.

The **Night light** feature in the **Display** setting is new in the Windows 10 Creators Update. This can be used to apply a warmer color for the computer's display to create a more restful environment, particularly at night time. Click on the **Night light settings** link to apply these settings.

41

- **Notifications & actions**. This contains options for selecting which notification icons appear on the Taskbar, and specifying which apps can be used to display notifications, e.g. your calendar and email.

- **Power & sleep**. This contains options for when the screen is turned off when not being used, and when the computer goes to sleep when it is not being used. This ranges from one minute to never.

...cont'd

- **Battery**. This can be used on laptops, and displays the charge level of the battery and what is using the battery most. It also has options for saving battery power.

- **Storage**. This displays how much storage has been taken up on your computer and has options for where you want to save certain types of content. This can be the PC or an external drive, such as a hard drive or a USB flashdrive.

- **Tablet mode**. This can be used on desktop and laptop computers, using a mouse and keyboard to replicate the operation of using a touchscreen device or tablet with Windows 10. This includes expanding the Start menu to full screen.

- **Multitasking**. This contains options for working with windows and desktops. In the **Snap** section you can turn on options for arranging windows when they are moved to the edge of the screen, and in the **Virtual desktops** section you can specify whether the Taskbar (and Alt + Tab) shows all open windows, or just those for the current desktop.

- **Projecting to this PC**. This can be used to allow other Windows 10 devices (computers, tablets or phones) to project their screens on to your computer so that you can view the screen and also interact with it.

- **Shared experiences**. This can be used to enable you to open your apps and content on other devices.

- **About**. This contains information about your computer and the version of Windows that you are using.

Devices Settings

The Devices Settings provide settings for how the hardware connected with your computer operates. They include:

- **Bluetooth & other devices**. This can be used to link your computer to compatible Bluetooth devices, so that they can share content over short distances with radiowaves. The two devices have to be 'paired' initially to be able to share content.

- **Printers & scanners**. This can be used to add new printers or scanners to your computer. These can either be wireless ones, or ones which connect via cable. In most cases, the required software will be installed with Windows 10, or if not, it will be downloaded from the internet.

- **Mouse**. This contains options for customizing the mouse. These include setting the main button (Left, by default) and how the scrolling operates with the mouse, such as the number of lines that can be scrolled at a time (Multiple by default).

Printers can also be added through the **Control Panel**. This is done in the **Devices and Printers** section, under **Hardware and Sound**. Click on the **Add a printer** button and follow the wizard.

- **Touchpad**. This contains options for customizing the touchpad (for a laptop).

- **Typing**. This contains options for correcting your typing as you go. These include autocorrecting misspelt words, and highlighting misspelt words.

- **Pen & Windows Ink**. This contains options for using a stylus to jot down notes, and sketch on the screen.

- **AutoPlay**. This contains options for applying AutoPlay for external devices such as removable drives and memory cards. If AutoPlay is On, the devices will be activated and accessed when they are attached to your computer.

- **USB**. This can be used to flag up any issues with connected USB devices.

...cont'd

Network & Internet Settings

The Network & Internet Settings provide settings related to connecting to networks, usually for accessing the internet. They include:

- **Status**. This displays the current Wi-Fi status, i.e. whether the computer is connected to the internet or not.

- **Wi-Fi**. This contains options for connecting to the internet via your Wi-Fi router (or public hotspots). There is also an option for managing your Wi-Fi networks.

- **Ethernet**. This can be used if you are connecting to the internet with an Ethernet cable. This connects to the Ethernet port on your computer, and internet access is delivered through the use of your telephone line.

- **Dial-up**. This can be used if you have a dial-up modem for connecting to the internet. This is not common these days, but is still a valid means of internet access.

- **VPN**. This can be used to connect to a corporate network over VPN (Virtual Private Network). If you are doing this, you will need certain settings and details from your network administrator.

- **Airplane mode**. This can be used to turn off wireless communication when you are on a plane, so that you can still use your computer (laptop) safely.

- **Mobile hotspot**. This can be used to determine how the computer interacts with mobile hotspots for connecting to shared public networks.

- **Data usage**. This displays how much data has been downloaded over any networks that you are using. The most common one is Wi-Fi, and displays your usage over a 30 day period.

- **Proxy**. This contains options for using a proxy server for Ethernet or Wi-Fi connections.

Don't forget

If Wi-Fi is turned **On** in the Wi-Fi settings, any routers in range should be recognized. A password will probably then be required to connect to the router.

Personalization Settings

The Personalization Settings provide options for customizing the look and feel of Windows 10. They include:

- **Background**. This can be used to change the Desktop background in Windows 10. You can select images from the pictures provided, solid colors, a slideshow, or your own photos (using the **Browse** button). You can also choose how the background fits the screen (the default is Fill).

- **Colors**. This contains options for selecting a color for borders, buttons, the Taskbar and the Start menu background.

- **Lock screen**. This can be used to select a background for the Lock screen. You can use the images provided and also select your own photos (using the **Browse** button). You can also select apps that display relevant information on the Lock screen, such as email notifications or calendar events.

In the Colors section there is also an option for making the Start menu, Taskbar and Action Center (Notifications) transparent. This is accessed beneath the color chart for selecting an accent color.

45

- **Themes**. This contains options for color themes that can be applied for several elements within the Windows 10 interface.

- **Start**. This contains options for how the Start menu operates. It can be used to view the Start menu in full screen mode and also display recently used items in the Start menu.

- **Taskbar**. This contains options for locking the Taskbar, automatically hiding it, changing the icon size, and specifying its screen location (left, top, right or bottom).

...cont'd

Apps Settings

The Apps Settings provide options for specifying how apps work and interact with Windows 10. They include:

- **Apps & features**. This contains information about the apps that you have on your computer. This includes their size and installation date. There is also an option to specify how apps can be downloaded to your computer. Click in the Installing apps box and select one of the options (**Allow apps from the Store only** is the most secure option.)

  > **Installing apps**
  >
  > Choose where you can get apps from. Installing only apps from the Store helps protect your PC and keep it running smoothly.
  >
  > Allow apps from anywhere ⌄
  >
  > ---
  >
  > Allow apps from anywhere
  >
  > Warn me before installing apps from outside the Store
  >
  > Allow apps from the Store only

Apps settings as a separate category is a new feature in the Windows 10 Creators Update.

The Accounts Settings can be used to switch between a Microsoft Account and a Local account for signing in to your PC.

- **Default apps**. This can be used to select default apps for opening certain items, such as email, music, photos and videos. Click on the **Choose a default button** next to a function to select a default app for it. Once a default app has been selected, it can be changed by clicking on the current default and selecting a new one.

  > **Choose default apps**
  >
  > Email
  >
  > [+] Choose a default
  >
  > Maps
  >
  > [◉] Maps
  >
  > Music player
  >
  > [◎] Groove Music

- **Offline maps**. This contains options for downloading maps so that you can use them even when you are offline. There is also an option for only downloading maps when you are connected to Wi-Fi, to save any unwanted charges if you have a mobile data plan.

- **Apps for websites**. This can be used to allow compatible apps to open websites, rather than using a browser.

Accounts Settings

The Accounts Settings provide options for adding new online accounts (such as a new email account, or an online storage and sharing service such as Dropbox). They include:

- **Your info**. This displays information about your current account, which will either be the one you signed in to using your Microsoft Account details, or a Local account, which has no online presence. You can also swap between accounts here.

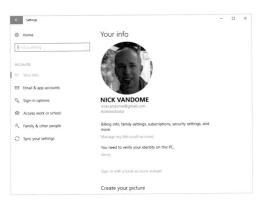

- **Email & app accounts**. This can be used to add email accounts and also add a Microsoft Account.

- **Sign-in options**. This contains security options for signing in to your account. You can create a PIN, Password or Picture password. Whichever method you choose, this will be required when you sign in to your account from the Lock screen.

- **Access work or school**. This can be used to connect to a workplace network, where you can share certain items. To do this you will need to contact the network administrator in order to obtain the correct settings to connect to the network.

- **Family & other people**. This can be used to set up accounts on your computer for other family members, or friends. They will be able to set their own sign-in options, and you will be able to switch users by clicking on the Start button and then clicking on the icon of the current user.

- **Sync your settings**. This can be used to sync the settings you have on your computer with any other Windows 10 devices that you have. For instance, if you have a desktop computer using Windows 10, you will be able to sync settings and apps with another Windows 10 device, such as a Surface tablet.

Don't forget

The Accounts Settings can be used to switch between a Microsoft Account and a Local account for signing in to your PC.

47

...cont'd

Time & Language Settings

The Time & Language Settings provide options for the time zone used by your computer and the format for these items. They include:

- **Date & time**. This can be used to set the date and time, either manually or automatically, using the **Time zone** drop-down menu. There is also a link to **Related settings** in the Control Panel, where formatting options can be applied.

[Settings window: Date & time]

Date & time

Date and time

2:09 PM, Friday, April 21, 2017

Set time automatically
On

Set time zone automatically
Off

Change date and time
Change

Time zone
(UTC+00:00) Dublin, Edinburgh, Lisbon, London

Adjust for daylight saving time automatically
On

Show additional calendars in the taskbar
Don't show additional calendars

- **Region & language**. This can be used to select the language that is used by your computer, e.g. English (United States). You can also add new languages.

[Settings window: Region & language]

Region & language

Country or region

Windows and apps might use your country or region to give you local content

United States

Languages

You can type in any language you add to the list. Windows, apps and websites will appear in the first language in the list that they support

+ Add a language

English (United States)
Windows display language

English (United Kingdom)
Language pack installed

- **Speech**. This contains options for how the speech function operates when using Windows 10. This includes the language to use when you are using speech, and also the default voice if using apps that speak text from the screen.

Don't forget

The date and time can be also be set within the **Clock, Language, and Region** section of the Control Panel, under the **Date and Time** heading.

Gaming Settings

The Gaming Settings contain a range of options:

- **Game bar**. This can be used for settings for the Game bar controller that can accessed when playing games with the Windows 10 Creators Update.

Gaming Settings is a new feature in the Windows 10 Creators Update.

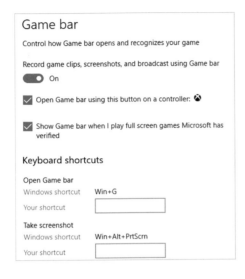

The Game bar is a new feature in the Windows 10 Creators Update.

The Game bar can be opened with keyboard shortcuts (WinKey + G by default), and it can be used to capture screenshots or video recording of the games being played. These can then be shared with other games players via the Xbox app. Click on this button on the Game bar to open the Xbox app.

Press and drag here on the Game bar to move it around the screen.

- **Game DVR**. This contains options for how screenshots and video of games being played are captured.

- **Broadcasting**. This contains settings for how games appear when they are broadcast to other gamers, through the Xbox app.

- **Game Mode**. This ensures the best possible gaming experience with Windows 10. Drag the **Use Game Mode** button **On** to activate it.

For more information about using the Xbox app and playing games with the Windows 10 Creators Update, see pages 181-182.

...cont'd

Ease of Access Settings

The Ease of Access Settings contain a range of options to help users who have visual or motor issues when using a computer. They include:

- **Narrator**. This can be used to activate a screen reader so text, buttons and toolbars can be read out loud. You can choose a voice style for the narrator, and the speed and pitch of reading.

- **Magnifier**. This can be used to magnify what is being viewed on the screen. The amount of magnification can be increased by up to 1600% of the standard view. The color of the screen can also be inverted.

- **High contrast**. This contains options for applying high contrast themes for Windows 10, to make certain elements more pronounced. This can be useful for users with dyslexia.

- **Closed captions**. This can be used by hearing-impaired users to provide text subtitles for items such as movies or multimedia content. The captioning is included in the media, and the settings enable you to select color, size and effects for the subtitles.

- **Keyboard**. This can be used to enable the on-screen keyboard, and options for keyboard shortcuts and keyboard sounds for when certain keys are pressed, e.g. Caps Lock and Number Lock.

Beware

The more access you give in terms of your own information and allowing apps to share your location, the more unwanted information you may be sent.

50

- **Mouse**. This contains options for setting the size of the mouse pointer and also its color.

- **Other options**. This contains options for turning Off animations and Windows backgrounds, to make the screen less distracting, and also options for showing notifications.

Privacy Settings

The Privacy Settings can be used to allow or deny certain apps access to your location. This can make them operate more efficiently, but you may not want all of your apps to function in this way. They include:

- **General**. This contains options for allowing or denying apps access to some of your personal information (such as name, picture and account info), using a SmartScreen Filter to check web pages used by certain apps, send Microsoft information about your typing, and allowing websites to provide you with local information based on your default language being used.

- **Location**. This can be used to turn On or Off the location services, to allow or deny apps the use of your location.

- **Notifications**. This can be used to specify which apps can show notifications in the Action Center and the Lock screen.

- The following options can be used to allow or deny apps access to these specific functions: **Camera**, **Microphone**, **Contacts**, **Calendar**, **Call history**, **Messaging** and **Radios**.

- **Speech, inking & typing**. This can be used to train Windows and the personal digital assistant, Cortana, to your writing and speaking styles, so that they can operate more efficiently.

- **Account info**. This can be used to allow apps access to your name, picture and account info.

- **Email**. This can be used to specify which apps can access email, e.g. the People app for using Contacts.

- **Tasks**. This can be used to specify which apps can access certain tasks being performed on your computer.

- **Other devices**. This can be used to view external devices, such as an Xbox, which have access to your apps.

- **Feedback & diagnostics**. This contains options for how feedback is requested by Microsoft. It can be set to automatically, or for a specific time period, e.g. once a week.

- **Background apps**. This can be used to specify which apps can receive notifications and updates even when not in use. This includes Mail and the Microsoft Edge browser.

There is also an option for **App diagnostics**, whereby apps can share diagnostic information in order to run as efficiently as possible.

...cont'd

Update & security

The Update & security Settings provide options for installing updates to Windows, and also backing up and recovering the data on your computer. They include:

- **Windows Update**. This can be used to install system updates, such as those to Windows 10, and also important security updates. They can be set to be checked for and installed automatically (using the **Advanced options** button) or manually using the **Check for updates** button. For some updates, your computer will shut down and restart automatically.

Don't forget

Because of the nature of Windows 10, e.g. it is designed as an online service, there will be regular updates. Check the Windows Update section regularly, even if you have set updates to be installed automatically, as you will be able to view the details of installed updates.

52

Settings	— □ ×
⚙ Home	**Windows Update**
Find a setting	Update status
Update & security	🔄 Your device is up to date. Last checked: Yesterday, 4:40 PM
↻ Windows Update	Check for updates
🛡 Windows Defender	Update history

Settings	— □ ×

⚙ **Advanced options**

Choose how updates are installed

☑ Give me updates for other Microsoft products when I update Windows.

☐ Use my sign in info to automatically finish setting up my device after an update.
Learn more

Privacy statement

Pause Updates

Temporarily pause updates from being installed on this device for up to 7 days. When updates resume, this device will need to get the latest updates before it can be paused again.

◯ Off

Pausing now will pause updates until 4/28/2017

Choose how updates are delivered

Note: Windows Update might update itself automatically first when checking for other updates.

Privacy settings

- **Windows Defender**. This contains options for protecting your computer with the Windows Defender app, including real-time protection and also Cloud protection for items that are stored online, such as in OneDrive.

- **Backup**. This can be used to back up your important files and documents. It is best if this is done to an external hard drive that is kept separately from your computer. Connect an external hard drive and click on the **Add a drive** button to start the process.

- **Recovery**. This can be used if you encounter problems with the way that Windows 10 is operating. You can select to refresh your computer and keep all of your files intact (although they should always be backed up first); reinstall Windows completely, which will reset it completely and you will lose all of your files and any apps you have downloaded; or return to an earlier version of Windows that was on your computer, without losing any files.

- **Activation**. This can be used to activate your copy of Windows 10, to confirm that it is an authorized version. Activation can be done online.

- **Find My Device**. This can be used to set up Find My Device for locating a lost device, via the website at: **account.microsoft.com/devices**

- **For developers**. This contains options for advanced users involved in programming and app development.

- **Windows Insider Program**. This can be used to gain access to the Insider Program, for downloading preview versions of the latest Windows 10 updates.

Searching

Searching for items and information on computers and the internet has come a long way since the first search engines on the web. Most computer operating systems now have sophisticated search facilities for finding things on your own computer as well as searching over the web. They also now have personal digital assistants, which are voice activated search functions, which can be used instead of typing search requests.

Windows 10 has a search box built-in to the Taskbar, which also includes the personal digital assistant, Cortana. This can also be used for a wide range of voice activated tasks.

Using the Search box for text searching

To use the Search box for text-only searches, over either your computer or the web:

1 Click in the Search box

2 Enter a search term (or website address)

3 Click on one of the results, or on the **See web results** button, to view the search results page in the Microsoft Edge browser

Hot tip

The top search result is displayed at the top of the window in Step 2.

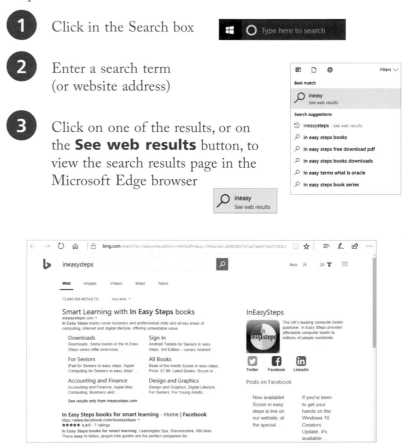

Asking a question

The Search box can also be used to ask specific questions:

 Enter a question in the Search box

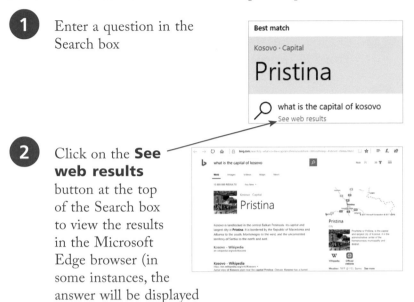

 Click on the **See web results** button at the top of the Search box to view the results in the Microsoft Edge browser (in some instances, the answer will be displayed at the top of the Cortana Search box too)

The magnifying glass icon indicates that a search is going to be undertaken on the web, and this will be displayed on a search results page, as in Step 2.

Searching over your computer

As well as searching over the web, the Search box can also be used to find items on your computer:

 Enter a search query into the Search box and click on one of the results to open the item on your computer

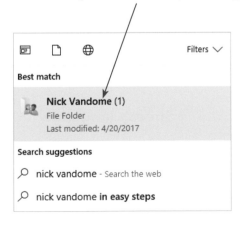

If you are searching for a keyword over files on your computer, the search will be conducted over the text in documents and folders, not just the document titles. It will also search over the online backup and storage facility, OneDrive, if you have this set up (see pages 162-165).

Setting Up Cortana

To ensure that you can use Cortana to perform voice searches and queries, the language settings on your Windows 10 computer have to be set up correctly. To do this:

1 Open the **Settings** app and click on the **Time & language** button

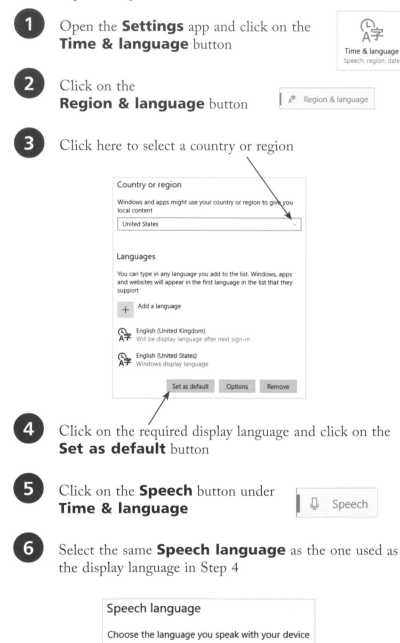

2 Click on the **Region & language** button

3 Click here to select a country or region

Country or region

Windows and apps might use your country or region to give you local content

United States

Languages

You can type in any language you add to the list. Windows, apps and websites will appear in the first language in the list that they support

+ Add a language

English (United Kingdom)
Will be display language after next sign-in

English (United States)
Windows display language

Set as default   Options   Remove

4 Click on the required display language and click on the **Set as default** button

5 Click on the **Speech** button under **Time & language**

🎤 Speech

6 Select the same **Speech language** as the one used as the display language in Step 4

Speech language

Choose the language you speak with your device

English (United States) ∨

The county or region, display language and speech language should be the same in order for Cortana to work.

If the Cortana Search box is not displayed once the languages have been set, restart your computer to apply the changes.

56

Using Cortana

Once the correct languages have been selected for Cortana, you have to ensure that your computer's microphone is working properly since it will be used for voice queries with Cortana.

Setting up the microphone
To set up your computer's microphone:

 Open the **Settings** app and click on the **Time & language** button

Time & language
Speech, region, date

 Click on the **Speech** button

🎤 Speech

3 Under the **Microphone** section, click on the **Get started** button

Microphone

Set up your mic for speech recognition

Get started

4 In the microphone wizard, click on the **Next** button

Beware

Most modern laptop computers have built-in microphones, but an external one may need to be attached to a desktop computer.

57

5 Repeat the phrase in the wizard window to complete setting up your microphone. (If the setup is successful, the wizard will move to the completion page automatically)

Beware

It can take Cortana a bit of time to fully recognize your voice and style of speech. Make sure that there is no loud background noise when you are using Cortana.

6 Click on the **Finish** button

Finish

Don't forget

You can right click in the Cortana Search box to select **Cortana** > **Show Cortana icon** (or **Show search box**).

Hot tip

Cortana can be used directly from the Lock screen, to ask general queries, such as 'What is the weather in my area?' or to play a song from the Groove Music app (see tip on page 61).

...cont'd

Voice searching with Cortana

As with text searches, Cortana can be used to search over various places and for different items:

1 Click on the microphone button in the Search box to begin a voice search

2 The Cortana symbol is displayed in the Search window with the word **Listening...** in the Search box. Say what you want to find

3 If Cortana cannot understand what you said, you are asked to try again

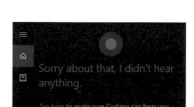

4 Cortana can be used to open specific apps, e.g. by saying "**Open Mail**"

5 If the query is general, e.g. "**Open Microsoft**", various options will be displayed

6 For a specific request, e.g. "**Open Microsoft Edge**", the required app will be opened

In the Windows 10 Creators Update, Cortana voice commands can be used to turn Off, Restart or put your PC to Sleep. They can also be used to change the system volume. Also, an increasing range of apps support Cortana, so can be used in conjunction with it, e.g. for playing movies with Netflix.

Text searches with Cortana

Once Cortana has been set up, text searches can be performed, and a range of other information can be displayed by Cortana.

1 Click in the Search box to start a text search

2 Before a search is started, Cortana displays a range of information it thinks is useful, such as the weather forecast and items from your calendar

...cont'd

Notebook options

The Notebook within Cortana can also be used to specify settings for a range of topics that are monitored by Cortana. These include items such as Eat & drink, Events, Finance, News, Sports and Travel. If the options are turned **On** you will automatically receive notifications and recommendations for these subjects.

 Click in the Search box and click on the **Notebook** button on the side toolbar. This displays the range of options, including **Connected Services**, **Eat & drink** and **Finance**

The items in the Notebook will, by default, be tailored to your geographical location.

60

 Click on an item to view its options, such as adding your Groove Music account so that Cortana can use this for searching and displaying music

Click on an item such as Eat & drink to turn **On** the cards so that Cortana can display recommendations and other items related to the subject

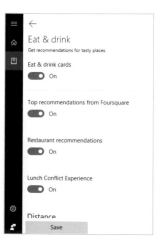

Cortana Settings

Settings for Cortana can be accessed from the Search window:

1 Click on the **Settings** button on the sidebar

2 Apply the Cortana Settings as required, including an option for Cortana to provide its own suggestions, and also setting Cortana to respond to saying "**Hey Cortana**" from any screen or app

Drag the **Use Cortana even when my device is locked** button to **On** to enable the use of Cortana from the Lock screen.

3 Scroll up the Settings window to access more options

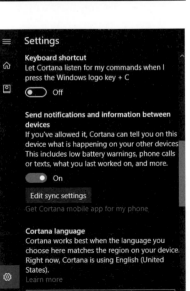

Setting Reminders

The Cortana Search box can also be used to set reminders that appear when required. To do this:

1 Click in the Search box and click on the **Notebook** button on the side toolbar

Notebook

ДΞ About Me

♀ Reminders

2 Click on the **Reminders** button

3 Click on this button to add a new reminder

4 Click in the **Remember to...** text box to add the item for which you want the reminder

5 Enter the reminder item details

Hot tip

If the Person or Place option is selected for a reminder, a specific person can be selected from your contacts in the People app, or a geographic location. These can also be used in conjunction with a specific time.

What do you want to be reminded about?

Reminder

Remember to...

Person | Place or | Time

Add a photo

Save | Cancel

6 Click in the **Time** text box to set a time for the reminder

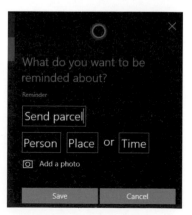

What do you want to be reminded about?

Reminder

Send parcel

Person | Place or | Time

Add a photo

Save | Cancel

7 Select a time for the reminder by clicking on the required item. Click on the **Another time...** button to set a custom time for the reminder

In 30 minutes

In 1 hour

Tomorrow

Another time...

NEW

Once a reminder has been set, click on the **Only once** box in Step 8 to select options for a recurring reminder. These include: every day, every day of the week, every month, or every week. This is a new feature in the Windows 10 Creators Update.

8 Enter any other criteria for the reminder and click on the **Remind** button

Remind you about this?

Reminder

Send parcel

3:21 PM

Today

Only once

Add a photo

Remind   Cancel

9 The details of the reminder are confirmed

Send parcel

3:21 PM   Today

Only once

Don't forget

To view completed reminders, click on the ... menu button at the bottom of the reminders window and click on the **History** button.

History

Select Add

10 When it is time for the reminder, it pops up from the Notification area on the Taskbar and also appears in the Cortana window

Remember to...
Send parcel
Today at 3:21 PM

Snooze for

5 minutes

Snooze   Complete

Adding and Switching Users

If more than one person uses the computer, each person can have a user account defined with a username and a password. To create a new user account, as either a Microsoft Account or a Local account:

 Access the **Settings** app and select **Accounts**

Accounts
Your accounts, email, sync, work, family

 Click on the **Family & other people** button

Accounts

R≡ Your info

✉ Email & app accounts

🔍 Sign-in options

🗄 Access work or school

🙎 Family & other people

 Click on the **Add a family member** button

Your family

You can allow family members to sign in to this PC. Adults can manage family settings online and see recent activity to help kids stay safe.

➕ Add a family member

64

Select whether the account is for a child or an adult. For a child, this provides online security options. Then, click Next

Add a child or an adult?

Enter the email address of the person you want to add. If they use Windows, Office, Outlook.com, OneDrive, Skype, or Xbox, enter the email address they use to sign in.

⦿ Add a child
    Kids are safer online when they have their own account
○ Add an adult

Enter their email address

The person I want to add doesn't have an email address

Next   Cancel

5 Enter the name of the new user, an email address and a password to create a Microsoft Account for the user

Let's create an account

Windows, Office, Outlook.com, OneDrive, Skype, Xbox. They're all better and more personal when they sign in with their Microsoft account. Learn more

After you sign up, we'll send you a message with a link to verify this user name.

lucyvandome17@gmail.com

Get a new email address

Password

United Kingdom

Birth month   Day   Year

Next   Back

6 Click on the **Next** button to complete the setup wizard

Next

7 The user is added to the Accounts page

Your family

You can allow family members to sign in to this PC. Adults can manage family settings online and see recent activity to help kids stay safe.

+ Add a family member

lucyvandome17@gmail.com   Can sign in
Child

Manage family settings online

Hot tip

Family Safety settings can be applied by clicking on the **Manage family settings online** link on the **Family & other people** page (see Step 7). This takes you to your online Microsoft Account page where settings can be applied for items such as web filtering, time controls and app restrictions.

8 Click on a user to change the type of their account, e.g. from a Local account to a Microsoft Account, or to delete their account

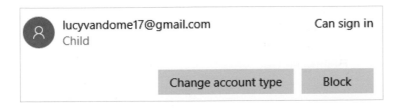

lucyvandome17@gmail.com   Can sign in
Child

Change account type   Block

...cont'd

Switching users

If you have a number of user accounts defined on the computer (several accounts can be active at the same time), you do not need to close your apps and log off to be able to switch to another user. It is easy to switch back and forth.

When switching users, all of your settings and files are maintained but the new user will not be able to see them, and you will not be able to see theirs when you switch back. Your screen should look exactly the same as you left it.

1 Click on the **Start** button

2 Click on your own user account icon and click on another user's name. They will have to enter their own password in order to access their account, at which point they will be signed in. You can then switch between users without each having to log out every time

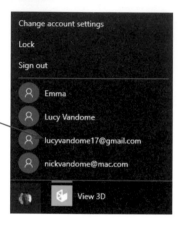

As an alternative way to switch users:

1 Press **WinKey** + **L** to lock the current user

2 Access the Log on screen for all of the current users and select one as required

Shut down

When you turn off your computer (see page 35), you will be warned if there are other user accounts still logged on to the computer.

Beware

If the other accounts have data files open, shutting down without logging them off could cause them to lose information.

1 Click on the **Shut down anyway** button to shut down without other users logging off

> Someone else is still using this PC. If you shut down now, they could lose unsaved work.
>
> **Shut down anyway**

66

3 Working with Apps

"Apps" is now a standard term in computing. Put simply, it is just another name for computer programs. In Windows 10, some apps are pre-installed, as with previous versions of Windows, while thousands more can be downloaded from the Windows Store. This chapter shows how to work with and organize apps in Windows 10, and how to find your way around the Windows Store.

Starting with Apps

The word "app" may be seen by some as a new-fangled piece of techno-speak. But, simply, it means a computer program. Originally, apps were items that were downloaded to smartphones and tablet computers. However, the terminology has now been expanded to cover any computer program. So, in Windows 10 most programs are referred to as "apps", although some legacy ones may still be referred to as "programs".

There are three clear types of apps within Windows 10:

- **Windows 10 apps**. These are the built-in apps that can be accessed from the Start menu. They cover the areas of communication, entertainment and information, and several of them are linked together through the online sharing service, OneDrive. In Windows 10, they open in their own window on the Desktop, in the same way as the older-style Windows apps (see below).

- **Windows classic apps**. These are the older-style Windows apps that people may be familiar with from previous versions of Windows. These open in the Desktop environment.

- **Windows Store apps**. These are apps that can be downloaded from the online Windows Store, and cover a wide range of subjects and functionality. Some Windows Store apps are free, while others have to be paid for.

Windows 10 apps

Windows 10 apps are accessed from the brightly-colored tiles on the Start menu (or listed on the left-hand side). Click on a tile to open the relevant app:

Don't forget

In Windows 10, all apps open directly on the Desktop and their operation is more consistent, regardless of the type of app.

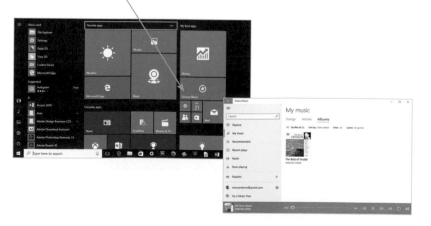

...cont'd

Windows classic apps

The Windows classic apps are generally the ones that appeared as default with previous versions of Windows, and would have been accessed from the Start button. The Windows classic apps can be accessed from the Start menu by using the alphabetic list, or searched for via the Taskbar Search box. Windows classic apps have the traditional Windows look and functionality, and they also open on the Desktop.

Some older Windows apps, such as Notepad and Paint, can be found in the Windows Accessories folder in the All apps alphabetic list. Alternatively, they can be searched for using the Cortana Search box.

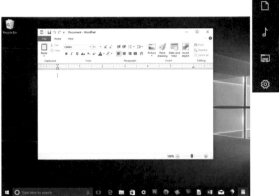

Windows Store apps

The Windows Store apps are accessed and downloaded from the online Windows Store. Apps can be browsed and searched for in the Store, and when they are downloaded they are added to the All apps alphabetic list on the Start menu.

The Windows Store is accessed by clicking on the **Store** tile on the Start menu or on the Taskbar.

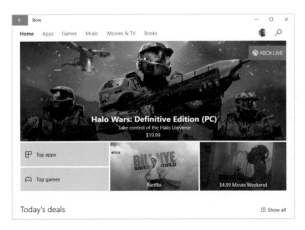

Windows 10 Apps

The Windows 10 apps that are accessed from the All apps alphabetic list on the Start menu cover a range of communication, entertainment and information functions. The apps include:

 Alarms & Clock. This provides alarms, clocks for times around the world, a timer and a stopwatch function.

 Calculator. This is a standard calculator that also has an option for using it as a scientific calculator.

 Calendar. This is a calendar which you can use to add appointments and important dates.

 Camera. This can be used to take photos directly onto your computer, but only if it has a built in camera.

 Connect. This can be used to connect a PC so that it can be used as a wireless projector.

 Cortana. This is the voice-activated personal digital assistant for Windows 10 to search for a variety of items.

 Groove Music. This can be used to access the online Music Store where music can be downloaded.

 Mail. This is the online Mail facility. You can use it to connect to a selection of email accounts.

 Maps. This provides online access to maps from around the world. It also shows traffic issues.

 Messaging. This can be used to send text messages to other users, using a Microsoft Account.

 Microsoft Edge. This is the default browser in Windows 10.

 Money. This is one of the information apps that provide real-time financial news, based on your location.

 Movies & TV (**Films & TV** in some regions). This is where you will see the movies and TV shows you buy in the Windows Store. There is also a link to the Video Store.

 News. This is one of the information apps that provide real-time news information, based on your location.

Don't forget

Some of these apps may not be supplied as standard on your Windows 10 system, but you can get them from the Windows Store (see pages 80-83).

Don't forget

See Chapter 9 for more information about working with the Microsoft Edge browser.

Don't forget

See Chapter 10 for more information about working with the Calendar, Mail, People and Skype apps, and how content can be shared between the different apps.

OneDrive. This is an online facility for storing and sharing content from your computer. This includes photos and documents.

 OneNote. This is a Microsoft note-taking app, part of the Office suite of apps.

 Paint 3D. This is an app that can be used to create, view and share 3D objects. For more details on using Paint 3D see pages 176-180.

 People. This is the address book app for adding contacts. Your contacts from sites such as Gmail and iCloud can also be imported into the People app.

 Photos. This can be used to view and organize your photos. You can also share and print photos directly from the Photos app.

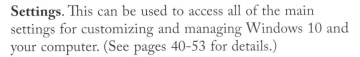 **Reader**. This can be used to open and view documents in different file formats, such as PDF and TIFF.

 Settings. This can be used to access all of the main settings for customizing and managing Windows 10 and your computer. (See pages 40-53 for details.)

 Sport. This is one of the information apps that provide real-time sports news, based on your location.

 Sticky Notes. This is an app for creating short notes that can be "stuck" to the screen, so that they are readily visible.

 Store. This provides access to the online Windows Store from where a range of other apps can be bought and downloaded to your computer.

 View 3D. This can be used to download and view 3D object that have been created by you or other people.

 Weather. This provides real-time weather forecasts for locations around the world. By default, it will provide the nearest forecast to your location.

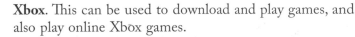 **Xbox**. This can be used to download and play games, and also play online Xbox games.

OneDrive can also be used to share your content, such as photos and documents, with other people. See pages 162-165 for details.

The information in the Money, News, Sports and Weather apps is provided by Bing.

There is a significant focus on 3D and Mixed Reality in the Windows 10 Creators Update. The **Mixed Reality Portal** app can be used to gain an overview of this technology.

Using Windows 10 Apps

In Windows 8 and 8.1, the newer style Windows apps had a different look and functionality. However, in Windows 10 all of the apps have been created with a more consistent appearance, although there are still some differences.

Windows 10 apps

Windows 10 apps open in their own window on the Desktop (in Windows 8 and 8.1 they only opened in full screen), and they can be moved and resized in the same way as older-style apps:

 Click and drag on the top toolbar to move the app's window

In Windows 10 there has been a conscious effort to achieve a greater consistency between the newer style apps and the old, classic style apps.

2 Drag on the bottom or right-hand border to resize the app's window (or the bottom right-hand corner to resize the height and width simultaneously)

Windows 10 app menus

Some Windows 10 apps have their own menus:

1 Click on this button (if available) within the app's window to access its menu

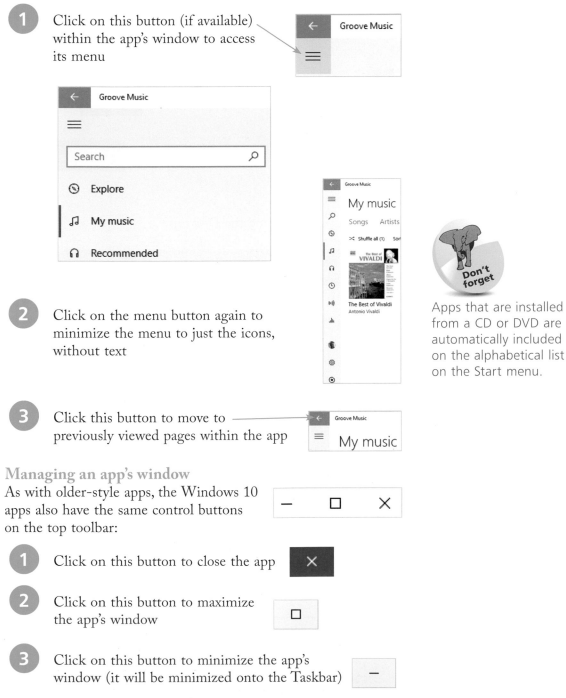

2 Click on the menu button again to minimize the menu to just the icons, without text

Don't forget

Apps that are installed from a CD or DVD are automatically included on the alphabetical list on the Start menu.

73

3 Click this button to move to previously viewed pages within the app

Managing an app's window

As with older-style apps, the Windows 10 apps also have the same control buttons on the top toolbar:

1 Click on this button to close the app

2 Click on this button to maximize the app's window

3 Click on this button to minimize the app's window (it will be minimized onto the Taskbar)

Classic Apps on the Desktop

The Windows classic apps open on the Desktop, in the same way as with previous versions of Windows, even though they are opened from the Start menu (or the Taskbar).

Opening a Windows classic app

To open a Windows classic app:

1 Click on the **Start** button and navigate through the app list

2 Select the app you want to open (for example WordPad, from the Windows Accessories section)

3 The app opens on the Desktop

Hot tip

If apps have been pinned to the Taskbar, as shown on page 79, they can be opened directly from there by simply clicking on them.

74

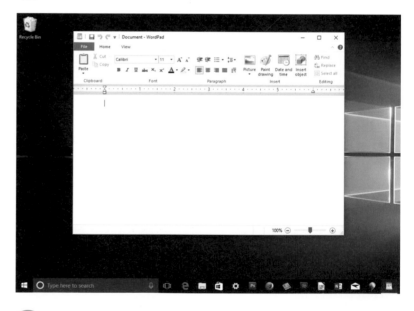

4 Click on the tabs at the top of the app to access relevant Ribbon toolbars and menus

Closing Apps

There are several ways to close a Windows app:

1 Click on the red **Close** button in the top right of the window

2 Select **File** > **Exit** from the File menu (if available)

3 Press **Alt** + **F4**

It is always worth saving a new document as soon as it is created. It should also be saved at regular intervals as you are working on it.

4 Right-click on the icon on the Taskbar and select **Close window**

5 If any changes have been made to the document, you may receive a warning message advising you to save the associated file

WordPad	✕
Do you want to save changes to Document?	
Save	Don't Save	Cancel

Viewing All Apps

There is a lot more to Windows 10 than the default Windows 10 apps. Most of the Windows apps that were available with previous versions of Windows are still there, and in the Windows 10 Creators Update, they are all available directly from the Start button, on the Start menu. To access all of the apps:

1 Click on the **Start** button

The All apps list can be hidden in the Windows 10 Creators Update. This is a new feature and can done in **Settings > Personalization > Start**. Drag the **Show app list in Start menu** button to **Off**. The apps list is minimized to the side of the screen. Click on this button to maximize the list (the button above it is for viewing the tiles on the Start menu).

2 All of the apps are displayed. Use the scroll bar to move through all of the apps, which are listed alphabetically

3 Click on a letter heading to view an alphabetic grid for finding apps. Click on a letter to move to that section

Searching for Apps

As you acquire more and more apps, it may become harder to find the ones you want. To help with this, you can use the Search box to search over all of the apps on your computer. To do this:

1 Click in the Search box on the Taskbar

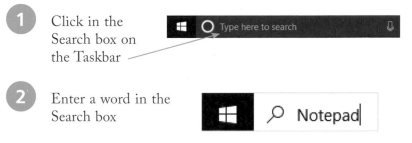

2 Enter a word in the Search box

3 As you type, relevant apps are displayed. When the one you are seeking appears, click on it to start the app

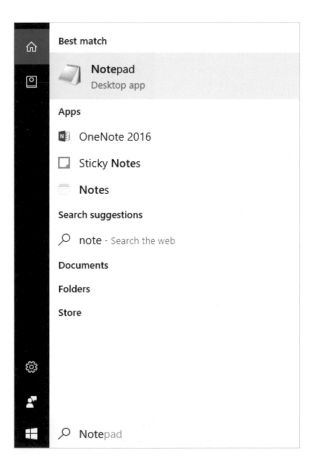

Hot tip

You just have to put in the first couple of letters of an app and Search will automatically suggest results based on this. The more that you type, the more specific the results become. Case does not matter when you are typing a search.

Pin to Start Menu

In most cases, you will want to have quick access to a variety of apps on the Start menu, not just the Windows 10 apps. It is possible to "pin" any app to the Start menu so that it is always readily available. To do this:

 Access the alphabetical list of apps, from the Start button

Hot tip

Apps can be unpinned from the Start menu by right-clicking on them and selecting **Unpin from Start** from the menu that appears.

2 Right-click on an app and click on the **Pin to Start** button

3 The app is pinned to the Start menu, in an unnamed group. It can now be repositioned, if required, as with any other app (see page 30)

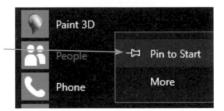

Pin to Taskbar

All apps can be pinned to the Desktop Taskbar (the bar that appears along the bottom of the Desktop), so that they can be accessed quickly. To do this:

 Click on the **Start** button to access the full list of apps

 Right-click on an app and click on **More** > **Pin to taskbar**

 The app is added to the Taskbar

Open apps on the Taskbar can also be pinned there by right-clicking on them and selecting **Pin to taskbar**

Pinned items remain on the Taskbar even once they have been closed

Hot tip

Apps can be unpinned from the Taskbar by right-clicking on them and selecting **More** > **Unpin from taskbar** from the contextual menu that appears.

79

Using the Windows Store

The third category of apps that can be used with Windows 10 are those that are downloaded from the Windows Store. These cover a wide range of topics, and they provide an excellent way to add functionality to Windows 10. To use the Windows Store:

1 Click on the **Store** tile on the Start menu

2 The currently featured apps are displayed on the Home screen

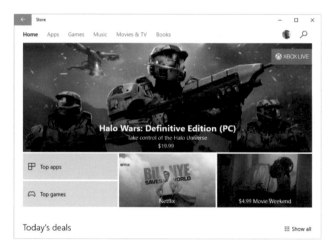

3 Scroll up and down to see additional featured apps

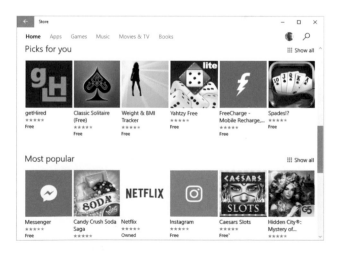

Click on the **Top apps** button on the Homepage and select apps under specific headings, e.g. **Best selling** apps

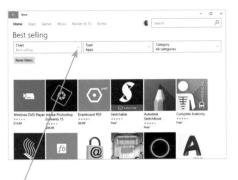

 Click here to select options for viewing apps according to certain criteria, e.g. **Top free**

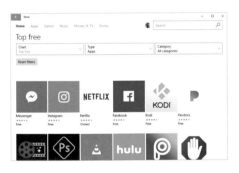

Click on an app to preview it, and for more details

Scroll up and down in Step 6 to view ratings and reviews about the app, and also any additional descriptions.

...cont'd

7 Click here to access the categories for apps

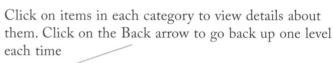

8 Click on a category to access it

9 Click on items in each category to view details about them. Click on the Back arrow to go back up one level each time

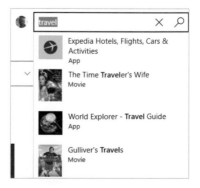

To return to the Home screen at any point, click on the **Home** button from the top toolbar.

10 Enter a word or phrase into the Search box to see matching apps. Click on a result to view the app

Buying Apps

When you find an app that you want to use, you can download it to your computer. To do this:

1 Access the app and click on the **Get** (or price) button

Adobe Photoshop Express
Adobe Systems Incorporated
★★★★ ☆ 669
Free*

Get   Share

+ Offers in-app purchases

2 The app downloads from the Windows Store and a **Downloading** message is displayed

Downloading . 13.29 MB of 13.29 MB

4.5 Mb/s

3 The app is added to the Start menu and has a **New** tag next to it. This disappears once the app has been opened

Ps Adobe Photoshop Express
New

4 Click on the app to open and use it (initially it will be available under the **Recently added** section of the Start menu, as well as its own alpha listing)

Recently added

Ps Adobe Photoshop Express

≡   Adobe Photoshop Express   ⤢ – □ ✕

Ps Adobe Photoshop Express

Select an image source to start editing

Pictures Library   Camera

Don't forget

If there is a fee for an app, this will be displayed instead of the **Get** button. You will need to have credit/debit card details registered on your Microsoft Account in order to buy paid for apps (**Settings > Accounts > Manage my Microsoft Account**).

Don't forget

Once apps have been downloaded they can be reorganized and moved into different groups on the Start menu, or dragged away from their default group to start a new one (see pages 30-31).

Viewing Your Apps

As you download more and more apps from the Windows Store you may lose track of which ones you have obtained and when. To help with this, you can review all of the apps you have downloaded, from within the Windows Store. To do this:

1 Open the Windows Store and click on your account picture button at the top of the screen

2 Click on the **Downloads and updates** button

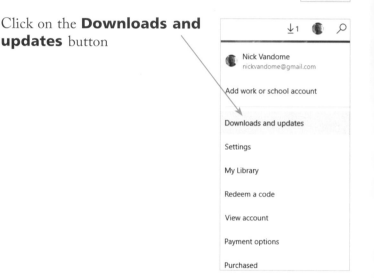

Nick Vandome
nickvandome@gmail.com

Add work or school account

Downloads and updates

Settings

My Library

Redeem a code

View account

Payment options

Purchased

3 All of the apps that have been downloaded are displayed. Tap on the **Check for updates** button to see if there are any updates for the listed apps

Don't forget

You can reinstall apps from the Downloads section, even if you have previously uninstalled them. If there was a fee for an app, you will not have to pay again to reinstall it.

Using Live Tiles

Before any of the Windows 10 apps have been used, they are depicted on the Start menu with tiles of solid color. However, once you open an app it activates the Live Tile feature (if it is supported by that app). This enables the tile to display real-time information from the app, even when it is not the app currently being used. This means that you can view information from your apps, directly from the Start menu. To use Live Tiles:

1 Right-click on a tile to select it. If it has Live Tile functionality, click on **More > Turn Live Tile on** to activate this feature

The apps with Live Tile functionality include Mail, People, Calendar, Photos, Groove Music, News, Sport and Money. Some of these, such as Mail, require you to first set up an account before Live Tiles can be fully activated.

2 Live Tiles display real-time text and images from the selected apps. These are updated when there is new information available via the app

3 To turn off a Live Tile, right-click on a tile to select it and click on **More > Turn Live Tile off**

If you have too many Live Tiles activated at the same time it can become distracting and annoying, with a lot of movement on the Start menu.

Install and Uninstall

Installing apps from a CD or DVD

If the app you want to install is provided on a CD or DVD, you normally just insert the disc. The installation app starts up automatically, and you can follow the instructions to select features and complete the installation. If this does not happen automatically:

You can access the Run function in Windows 10 by right-clicking on the **Start** button and selecting **Run** from the contextual menu.

1 Insert the disc and click on this notification window

DVD RW Drive (D:) CS5 Design Prem1 ✕
Tap to choose what happens with this disc.

2 Double-click on the **Set-up.exe** file link to run it. Follow the on-screen prompts to install the app

DVD RW Drive (D:) CS5 Des...

Choose what to do with this disc.

Install or run program from your media

Run Set-up.exe
Published by Adobe Systems Incorporated

Other choices

Import pictures and videos
Dropbox

Open folder to view files
File Explorer

Take no action

Apps can also be installed from discs from File Explorer. To do this, locate the **Set-up.exe** file and double-click on it to start the installation process in the same way as in Step 2.

3 Apps that are installed from a CD or DVD are added to the All apps list on the Start menu

A

Access 2016

Acer

Adobe Design Premium CS5

Br Adobe Bridge CS5

Adobe Device Central CS5

Dw Adobe Dreamweaver CS5

Adobe ExtendScript Toolkit CS5

Adobe Extension Manager CS5

Id Adobe InDesign CS5

...cont'd

Uninstalling apps

In some previous versions of Windows, apps were uninstalled through the Control Panel. However, in Windows 10 they can also be uninstalled directly from the Start menu. To do this:

 Right-click on an app to access its menu

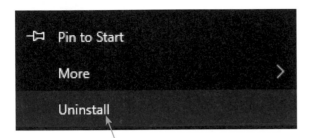

Don't forget

To get to the Control Panel, click on the **Start button**, scroll down to **Windows system**, click on the Down arrow and then select **Control Panel**.

2 Click on the **Uninstall** button

3 A window alerts you to the fact that related information will be removed if the app is uninstalled. Click on the **Uninstall** button if you want to continue

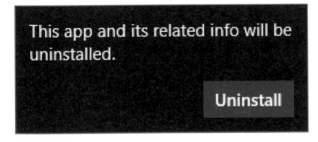

Don't forget

Some elements of Windows 10, such as the Control Panel, still refer to apps as programs, but they are the same thing.

4 If the app is a new Windows 10 one, or has been pinned to the Start menu (or Taskbar), its tile will be removed from its pinned location(s). For other apps, they will no longer be available from the list of apps

If apps have been installed from a CD or DVD they can also still be uninstalled from within the Control Panel. To do this, select the **Programs** section and click on the **Uninstall a Program** link. The installed apps will be displayed. Select one of the apps and click on the **Uninstall/Change** link.

Task Manager

Task Manager lists all the apps and processes running on your computer; you can monitor performance or close an app that is no longer responding.

To open the Task Manager:

 Right-click on the **Start** button and select **Task Manager**, or press **Ctrl** + **Shift** + **Esc**

Don't forget

As an alternative, press **Ctrl** + **Alt** + **Delete** to display the Windows Security screen, from where you can start Task Manager.

2 When Task Manager opens, details of the currently running apps are displayed

3 If an app is given the status of Not Responding and you cannot wait for Windows to fix things, select the app and click on the **End task** button

Beware

If an app stops responding, Windows 10 will try to find the problem and fix it automatically. Using Task Manager to end the app may be quicker, but any unsaved data will be lost.

4 Click on the **More details** button to view detailed information about the running apps. Select the **Processes** tab to show the system and the current user processes

5 The total CPU usage and the amount being used by each process are shown as (continually varying) percentages

6 Select **Performance** to see graphs of resource usage

7 The Performance panel shows graphs of the recent history of CPU and memory usage, along with other details

Alternative view

In addition to the standard view, with menus and tabs, Task Manager also has a CPU graph only view:

1 To switch to the graph only view, double-click the graph area on the Performance tab

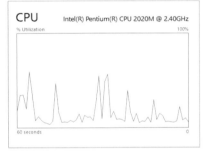

2 To switch back to the view with menus and tabs, double-click the graph area a second time

3 Select the **Wi-Fi** button in the Performance section to view the activity on your local area network. This tab also offers a graph only view

Hot tip

Resize the window (see page 97) so it does not take up too much space on your screen, and you can see the effects on CPU and memory as you use your system.

89

Don't forget

If you have a network adapter fitted to your computer, the Task Manager will feature a Networking tab.

Resource Monitor

The Resource Monitor provides an even more detailed view of the activities on your computer, and can be an essential aid in troubleshooting. To start the Resource Monitor:

1 From Task Manager, **Performance** tab, select the **Open Resource Monitor** button

Hot tip

Right-click any process and choose **Analyze Wait Chain...** to see which tasks are holding up an unresponsive application.

Ⓝ Open Resource Monitor

2 This displays CPU, Memory, Disk and Network details

3 For even more detail, select one of the tabs, e.g. Memory

4 Standard Controls

Even in Windows 10, much of what you do will be with menus, dialog boxes and windows, as used in numerous versions of the operating system. This chapter shows how to use these elements and how you can control and manage working with folders and files in Windows 10.

Menus

Traditionally, windows have a tabbed Menu bar near the top, displaying the menu options relevant to that particular window. Some Menu bars consist of drop-down menus, and others are in the format of the Ribbon, also known as the Scenic Ribbon.

Drop-down menus

For apps such as Notepad and WordPad, the Menu bar consists of tabbed drop-down menus:

 Open the app and click or tap on one of the Menu bar options to view its details

The Menu bar is not always displayed in folder windows. Press the **Alt** key to display it temporarily.

The ellipse (i.e. **...**) indicates that if this option is selected, an associated window with further selections will be displayed.

Scenic Ribbon

For apps such as WordPad (and also File Explorer and Office apps) there is a Ribbon (or Scenic Ribbon) at the top of the window with the Menu bar tabs:

 Open the app and select one of the Menu bar tabs on the Ribbon to view its details

Some options may have shortcut keys associated with them (e.g. **Alt** + **Up arrow** – Up one level), so you can use these instead of using your mouse. Other examples of shortcut keys are:

Ctrl + **A** – Select All   **Ctrl** + **C** – Copy   **Ctrl** + **V** – Paste
Ctrl + **X** – Cut   **Ctrl** + **Y** – Redo   **Ctrl** + **Z** – Undo

If an option is grayed (dimmed out), it is not available for use at this particular time or is not appropriate.

92

Dialog Boxes

Although simple actions can be made quickly from menu options, more specific settings are made from windows displayed specifically for this purpose. These are called dialog boxes.

Tabs
Some dialog boxes are divided into two or more tabs (grouped options). Only one tab can be viewed at a time.

Check boxes
Select as many as required. A tick indicates that the option is active. If you select it again it will be turned off. If an option is grayed, it is unavailable and you cannot select it.

Radio buttons
Only one out of a group of radio buttons can be selected. If you select another radio button, the previously-selected one is automatically turned off.

Command buttons
OK will save the settings selected and close the dialog box or window. **Cancel** will close, discarding any amended settings. **Apply** will save the settings selected so far but will not close, enabling you to make further changes.

Dialog boxes are usually fixed-size windows and therefore do not have scroll bars, minimize and maximize buttons or resize pointers.

These examples are from the Folder Options dialog box. To access it, select **Options** on the View section of the Ribbon in File Explorer and select **Change folder and search options**.

Structure of a Window

You can have a window containing icons for further selection, or a window that displays a screen from an app. All these windows are similar in their structure. This example is from the File Explorer.

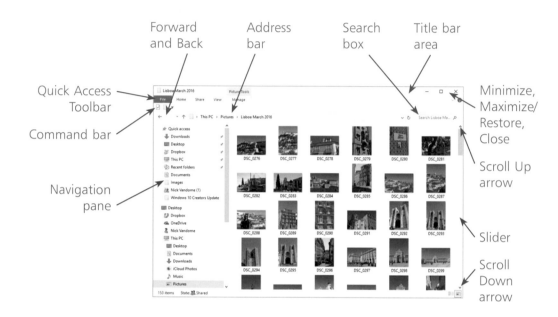

Scroll bars will only appear when there are items that cannot fit into the current size of the window. Here, only a vertical scroll bar is needed.

If you move the mouse pointer over any edge of a window, the pointer changes shape and becomes a double-headed Resize arrow – drag it to change the size of a window (see page 97).

Double-click on an icon to open a window relating to it – in this case a WordPad application window. This window has a Quick access toolbar, Menu bar, Ribbon, ruler, and a Control icon at the top left.

Moving a Window

As long as a window is not maximized, i.e. occupying the whole screen, you can move it. This is especially useful if you have several windows open and need to organize your Desktop.

1 Move the mouse pointer over the Title bar of a window

You will see the whole window move, with the full contents displayed and transparency still active while you are dragging the window.

2 Drag the mouse pointer across the Desktop (left-click and hold, or tap and hold as you move)

3 When the window reaches the desired location, release to relocate the window there

If you have two monitors attached to your system, you can extend your Desktop onto the second monitor and drag a window from one monitor onto the other.

Control menu Move
There is a Move command for the window on the Control menu.

1 Right-click the Title bar and select **Move**, and the mouse pointer changes to a four-headed arrow

2 Click on the window, holding down the left mouse button and moving the pointer towards the Title bar

3 The mouse pointer changes to an arrow, grabs the window and you can move and drop it as above

If the Title bar has a Control icon, left-click this to show the menu.

	Lisboa March 2016	
⊡	Restore	
	Move	
	Size	
—	Minimize	
◻	Maximize	
×	**Close**	Alt+F4

Restoring a Window

Within the Desktop environment there are a number of actions that can be performed on the windows within it. A window can be maximized to fill the whole screen, minimized to a button on the Taskbar or restored to the original size.

You can also double-click or tap the **Title bar** to maximize the window. Repeat the process to restore it to the original.

You can also use Snap Assist to maximize, move or resize windows (see pages 100-101).

Original size window   Maximize button   Maximized window

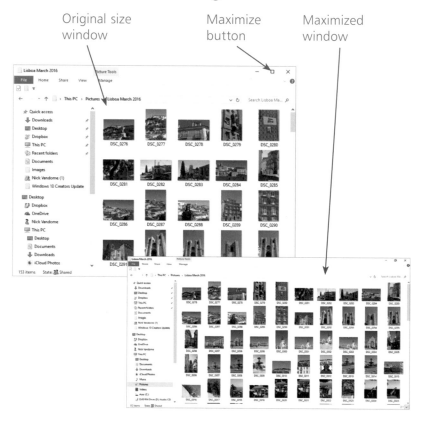

You can right-click the Title bar area or left-click the **Control** icon, to display the Control context menu (see next page).

Whether a window is maximized or original size, click on the **Minimize** button (left of the top-right three buttons) to reduce the window to its Taskbar icon. This will create space on the Desktop for you to work in other windows. When you want to restore the reduced window, simply select its **Taskbar** icon.

The middle button is the Maximize button. Or, if the window is already maximized, the button changes to the Restore button.

Click **Close**, the third button, when you want to close an app or to close a window.

Resizing a Window

If a window is not maximized or minimized, it can be resized.

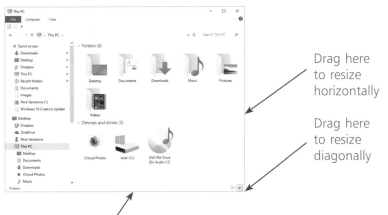

Drag here to resize horizontally

Drag here to resize diagonally

Drag here to resize vertically

Hot tip

Resize and move all of the windows on your Desktop to organize the layout to the way you prefer to work, or see pages 98-99 for other ways of arranging windows.

1 Place the mouse arrow anywhere on the edge of a window or on any of the corners. The pointer will change to a double-headed Resize arrow

2 Click, or tap, and drag the arrow outwards to increase the size of the window, or inwards to reduce the size

Control menu Size

There is a Size command on the Control menu which makes it easier to grab the edge of the window.

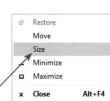

	Restore
	Move
	Size
	Minimize
	Maximize
x	Close Alt+F4

Beware

The Size command is not available if the window is maximized.

1 Right-click the Title bar (or left-click the Control icon) and select **Size**

2 The mouse pointer changes to a four headed arrow

3 Click the window, holding down the left mouse button, and move the pointer towards an edge or a corner of the window

4 The mouse pointer changes to a double-headed arrow and grabs the edge or corner, so you can stretch the window to the desired size, then release

Arranging Windows

If you have several windows open on your Desktop and you want to automatically rearrange them neatly, rather than resize and move each one individually, use the Cascade or Tile options.

Beware

Only open windows are arranged, not minimized windows. Also, fixed-size windows will get a proportional share of the screen, but they will not be resized.

 Right-click a clear area on the Taskbar to display a context menu and select one of the arrangement options

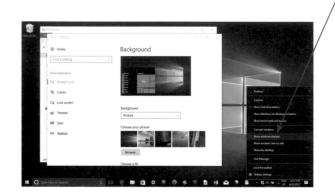

98

Don't forget

When you right-click the Taskbar, all windows are deselected, so you must click or tap a window to select it and make it currently active.

 Cascade windows overlaps all open windows, revealing the Title bar areas and resizing the windows equally

Hot tip

When you have used a function to arrange windows, a matching Undo function is added to the Taskbar context menu.

 Show windows stacked resizes windows equally and displays them across the screen in rows

Cascade windows

Show windows stacked

Show windows side by side

Show the desktop

Undo Cascade all windows

Show windows side by side resizes windows equally and displays them across the screen in columns

...cont'd

When you have a number of windows open on the Desktop, you might wish to see what is hidden underneath. For this, Windows 10 offers the Peek function.

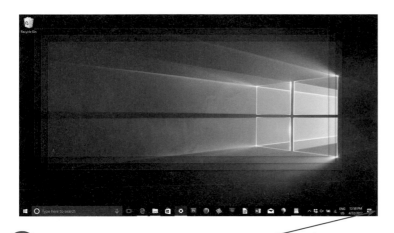

1 Right-click on the **Show desktop** area and select **Peek at desktop**. This will reveal outlines of the open apps whenever the cursor is moved over the Show desktop area

66

2 Select the **Show desktop** option in Step 1 to show just the desktop when the cursor is moved over the Show desktop area

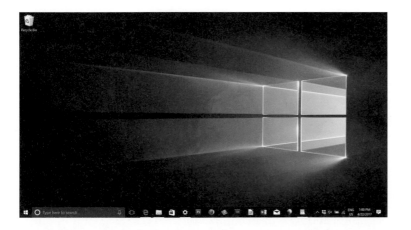

Snap Assist

Snap Assist provides a set of methods for resizing and moving windows around the Desktop.

Maximize fully

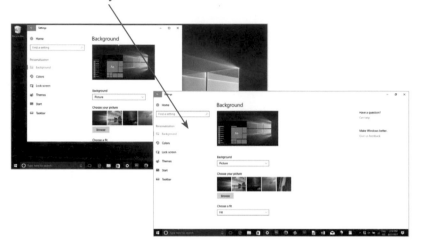

If the window you want to maximize is not the current one, click on it first before carrying out the Maximize operation.

Click, or tap, and hold the Title bar and drag the window up the screen. As the mouse pointer reaches the top edge of the screen, the window maximizes. The shortcut is **WinKey** + **Up Arrow**.

Maximize vertically

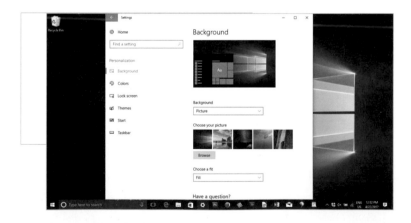

Alternatively, you can drag the bottom border of the window towards the bottom edge of the screen.

Click or tap and hold the top border of the window (until it turns into a double-headed arrow), and drag it towards the top edge of the screen. When the mouse pointer reaches the edge of the screen, the window will maximize in the vertical direction only. The shortcut is **WinKey** + **Shift** + **Up Arrow**.

Snap to the left

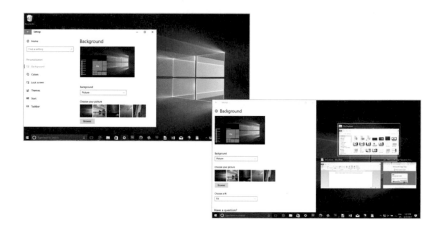

When you click the Title bar on an app such as WordPad, be sure to avoid the tools on the Quick access toolbar.

To position the window to fill the left-hand side of the screen, click, or tap, the Title bar and drag it to the left. As the mouse pointer reaches the left edge, the window resizes to fill half of the screen. The shortcut is **WinKey** + **Left Arrow**.

Snap to the right

To position the window to fill the right-hand side of the screen, click or tap the Title bar and drag it to the right. As the mouse pointer reaches the right edge, the window resizes to fill half of the screen. The shortcut key is **WinKey** + **Right Arrow**.

Hot tip

Alternatively, to make the two windows the only open (not minimized) windows, right-click the Taskbar, and then choose the option to **Show windows side by side**.

Compare two windows

Snap one of the windows to the left and the other window to the right.

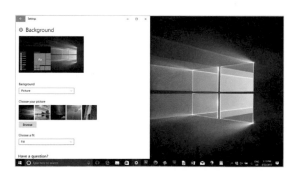

Restore

Drag the Title bar of a maximized or snapped window away from the edge of the screen and the window will return to its previous size (though not the same position). The shortcut is **WinKey** + **Down Arrow**.

Hot tip

Double-clicking or tapping the Title bar will also reverse the maximize or snap. This restores size and position.

Using Multiple Windows

Windows 10 provides great flexibility when it comes to working with windows: it is possible to display up to four active windows at a time, rather than just two side-by-side: To do this:

 Open an app and drag its window to the left-hand side of the screen, until it snaps left and takes up the left half of the screen

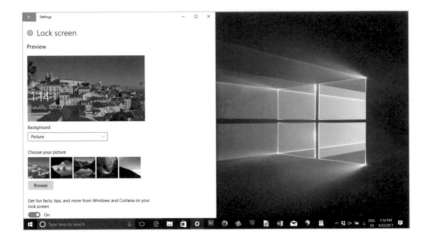

Apps can be arranged in multiple windows in any order, e.g. one can be placed in the right-hand corner and then one on the left-hand side.

 Open a second app and drag its window to the right-hand side of the screen, until it snaps right and takes up the right half of the screen

Open a third app and drag its window into the top left-hand corner of the screen. The left-hand side of the screen will display the two apps

4 Open a fourth app and drag its window into the top right-hand corner of the screen. The right-hand side of the screen will display the two apps

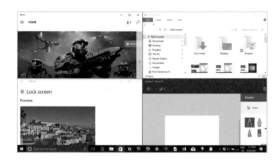

Don't forget

Apps can be 'unsnapped' from their positions, by clicking and holding on the Title bar and dragging them into a new position.

5 If other apps are open when an app is snapped into position, the Task View will display these apps in the space on the Desktop. Click on an app to expand it to fill the available space

Switching Windows

If you have several windows open on your Desktop, only one will be active. This will be the foremost window and it has its Title bar, Menu bar and outside window frame highlighted. If you have more than one window displayed on the Desktop, select anywhere inside a window that is not active to activate it and switch to it.

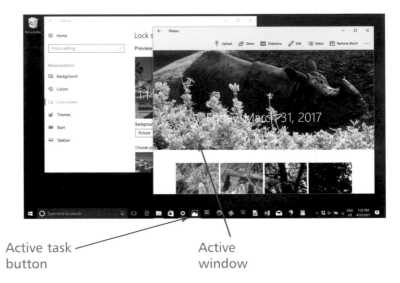

Active task —
button

Active
window

Another method of switching windows is to use the Taskbar at the bottom. Every window that is open has an icon button created automatically on the Taskbar. Therefore, it does not matter if the window you want to switch to is overlaid with others and you cannot see it. Just select the button for it in the Taskbar and the window will be moved to the front and made active.

Move the mouse pointer over a task button, and a Live Preview is displayed (one for each window if there are multiple tasks).

Don't forget

You can click on the preview to select that item and bring its window to the front of the Desktop.

Arranging Icons

You can rearrange the order of the items in your folders or on
your Desktop in many different ways.

 Right-click in a clear area (of the Desktop or folder
window) to display a shortcut context menu

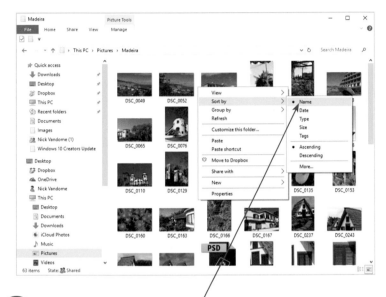

Select the **View** button
to cycle through a range
of views. Click or tap the
Down arrow to see
the full set of options.

Hot tip

105

Move the pointer over **Sort by** to reveal the submenu
of sorting options and click or tap the **Name** option, for
example, to sort all the file icons in ascending name order

Select **Name** a second time and the files will be sorted
in descending name order

Group by

You can select **Group by** for
folder windows (but not for the
Desktop). This groups your files
and folders alphabetically by
name, size, type, etc.

Closing a Window

When you have finished with a window you will need to close it. There are several ways of doing this – use the method that is easiest and the most appropriate at the time.

Open window

If the top right corner of the window is visible on the Desktop:

Don't forget

Save your work before closing any app window in which you have been working. However, Windows will prompt you if you forget.

1 Select the **Close** button on the Title bar

Minimized window

For a window that is minimized or one that is hidden behind other windows:

1 Move the mouse pointer over the associated Taskbar icon button

2 Select the **Close** button on the Live Preview for the task

Control menu

If only part of the window is visible on the Desktop:

1 Select the **Control** icon (top left corner) or right-click the Title bar

2 Select **Close** on the Control menu

Keyboard

To close any type of window, use this key combination:

1 Select the window to make it the current, active window, then press **Alt** + **F4** to close the window

5 Customizing Windows

The Desktop environment is still an important one in Windows 10, and this chapter looks at how to work with it and personalize it to your own requirements and preferences, with colors, themes and sounds.

Personalization

Customizing the look and feel of Windows 10 is a good way to feel like it is your own personal device. This can be done with some of the options in the Personalization section of the Settings app. To do this:

 Open the **Settings** app and click on the **Personalization** button

Personalization
Background, lock screen, colors

 Click on the **Background** button to select a Desktop background. Select **Picture** in the Background box and click to select a picture or click on the **Browse** button to select one of your own pictures

Click in the **Choose a fit** box in Step 2 to specify how the picture fills the background screen. The options are: Fill, Fit, Stretch, Tile, Center and Span.

Background

Home

Find a setting

Personalization

Background

Colors

Lock screen

Themes

Start

Taskbar

Background

Picture

Choose your picture

Browse

Choose a fit

Fill

 Click on the **Colors** button to select an accent color for the current background, Start menu and Taskbar

Colors

Home

Find a setting

Personalization

Background

Colors

Lock screen

Themes

Start

Taskbar

Sample Text

Choose your color

Automatically pick an accent color from my background

Recent colors

Windows colors

4 Check this box to **Off** to disable the automatic selection for the accent color

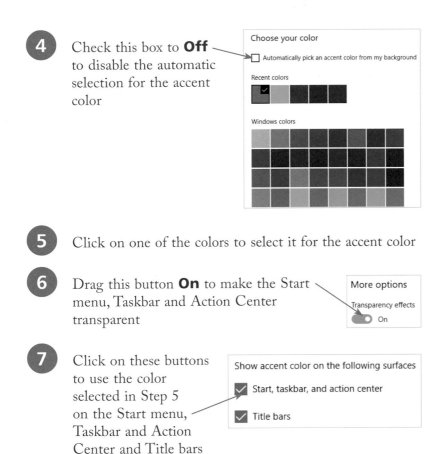

5 Click on one of the colors to select it for the accent color

6 Drag this button **On** to make the Start menu, Taskbar and Action Center transparent

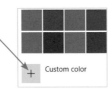

7 Click on these buttons to use the color selected in Step 5 on the Start menu, Taskbar and Action Center and Title bars

8 Click on the **Custom color** button underneath the color palette

Color customization is a new feature in the Windows 10 Creators Update.

9 Click on the color graph to select a customized accent color. Drag the slider underneath the graph to amend the selected color

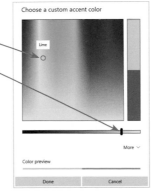

10 Click on the **Done** button to use the color selected in Step 9

Lock Screen Settings

The Settings app enables you to set the appearance of the Lock screen, the Start menu and select an account photo. To do this, first access the Settings:

1 Open the **Settings** app and click on the **Personalization** button

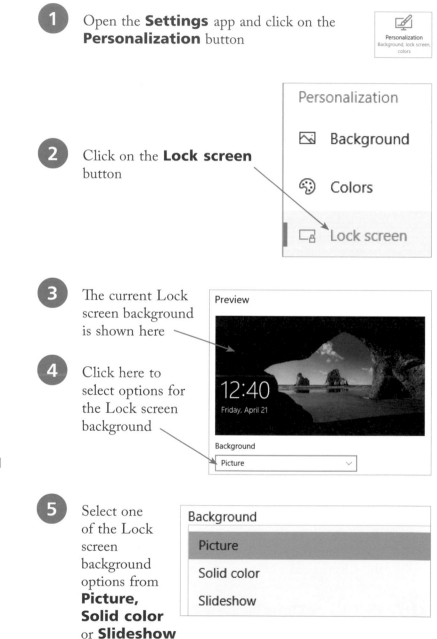

2 Click on the **Lock screen** button

3 The current Lock screen background is shown here

4 Click here to select options for the Lock screen background

5 Select one of the Lock screen background options from **Picture, Solid color** or **Slideshow**

Don't forget

If **Slideshow** is selected in Step 5, you will then have the option to choose an album of photos to use as the slideshow for the Lock screen background.

6 For the Picture option, click on the **Browse** button to select your own picture

7 Select an image and click on **Choose picture** to add this to the background options for the Lock screen

Hot tip

8 Other options for the Lock screen include selecting apps that display their detailed or quick status, options for screen timeout when not in use, and Screen saver settings

If you use your own images for the Lock screen background, these will remain available on the thumbnail row even if you switch to another image for the background.

Using Themes

Themes in the Windows 10 Creators Update can be used to customize several items for the look and feel of Windows:

1 Open **Setting** and select click on the **Personalization** button

2 Click on the **Themes** button

3 The current theme is displayed

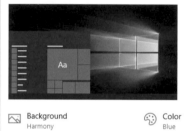

Using themes has been amended in the Windows 10 Creators Update.

4 Make a selection for a customized theme, using **Background**, **Color**, **Sounds** and **Mouse cursor**

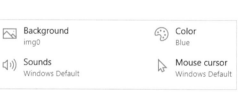

5 The selections for the customized theme are shown in the **Current theme** preview window

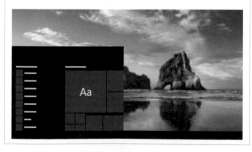

6 Click on the **Save theme** button to use it for the current theme

7 Click on one of the preset themes to select it rather than customizing one

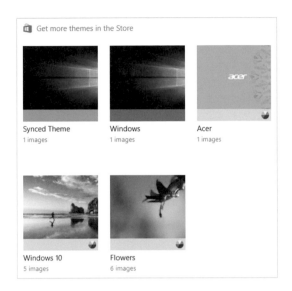

8 All of the elements of the preset theme are displayed in the preview window

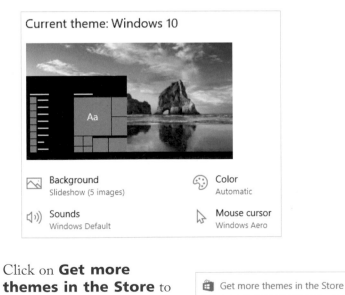

9 Click on **Get more themes in the Store** to download more themes that can be used on your PC

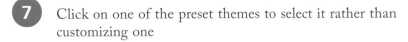

Changing Sound

1 Select **Settings** > **Personalization** > **Themes**

 Themes

2 Click on the **Sounds** button and click on the Sounds tab in the Sound window

 Sounds
Windows Default

Click the Down arrow on the Sound Scheme drop-down bar to try out a different scheme.

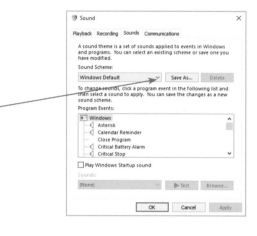

3 Select a Program Event and click the **Test** button to hear the associated sound

If you do not want to have sounds associated with Windows events, select **No Sounds** from the options in the drop-down list in Step 1.

4 Browse to locate a new sound file (file type .wav), then select **Test** to preview the effect

5 Make any other changes, then select **Save As...**, and provide a name for your modified sound scheme

Desktop Icons

To control the display of icons on the Desktop:

1 Right-click on the Desktop, click **View** and select **Show desktop icons**. A check mark is added

You can use the scroll wheel on your mouse to resize desktop icons. On the Desktop, hold down **Ctrl** as you roll the wheel up or down.

2 To resize the icons, display the View menu as above and click **Large icons**, **Medium icons** or **Small icons**

3 To remove the check mark and hide all the icons, display the View menu and select **Show desktop icons** again

When you right-click the Desktop, you will find customization functions, **Display settings** and **Personalize** on the context menu displayed.

4 To choose which of the system icons appear, open **Settings** and select **Personalization > Themes > Desktop icon settings** (under **Related Settings**)

5 Select or clear the boxes to show or hide icons as required, then click **Apply** and **OK** to confirm the changes

The **Control Panel** is one of the options in Step 5 and a link to it can be added to the Desktop in this way.

115

Screen Resolution

If you have a high resolution screen, you may find that the text, as well as the icons, are too small. You can increase the effective size by reducing the screen resolution.

If you want to use the Snap function as shown on pages 100-101 you need to have a minimum screen resolution of 1366 x 768.

1 Open the **Settings** app, select **System** and then click on the **Display** button

☐ Display

2 Drag this slider to change the overall brightness of items on your screen

Display
Brightness and color
Change brightness

Night light (off until 8:36 PM)
On
Night light settings

Scale and layout
Change the size of text, apps, and other items
100% (Recommended)
Custom scaling
Resolution
1366 × 768 (Recommended)
Orientation
Landscape

3 Click the drop-down arrow next to **Orientation** to switch the view to **Portrait**, e.g. for tablet PCs

If you have an LCD monitor or a laptop computer, you are recommended to stay with the native resolution, normally the highest.

4 Click here to change the screen resolution. Select a new resolution value from the list

Resolution
1366 × 768 (Recommended)

Resolution

1366 × 768 (Recommended)

1360 × 768

1280 × 768

1280 × 720

1280 × 600

1024 × 768

800 × 600

Detect

5 Click on the **Keep changes** button to change the screen resolution

Managing Storage

Computer storage is sometimes a feature that is taken for granted and left untouched. However, with the Windows 10 Creators Update there are some options for customizing how storage functions on your computer. To use these:

 Open the **Settings** app, select **System** and then click on the **Storage** button

2 At the top of the window, the current storage is displayed, with the amount used shown by a colored bar

Local storage

This PC (C:)
163 GB used out of 698 GB

3 Drag the **Storage sense** button to **On** to enable Windows to free up storage space by deleting redundant files and items in the Recycle Bin

Storage sense is a new feature in the Windows 10 Creators Update.

Storage sense

Windows can automatically free up space by getting rid of files you don't need, like temporary files and content in your recycle bin

On

4 Under the **More storage settings** heading, click on **Change where new content is saved**

More storage settings

Change where new content is saved

5 Select options for where new items will be saved (this can be used if you are using more than one drive)

Change where your apps, documents, music, pictures and videos are saved by default.

New apps will save to:

This PC (C:)

New documents will save to:

This PC (C:)

Ease of Access

Making Windows 10 accessible for as wider a range of users as possible is an important consideration, and there are a range of accessibility settings that can be used for this. To do this:

 Open **Settings** and click on the and click on the **Ease of Access** button

Don't forget

The settings for the Narrator can be used to specify the items on the screen that are read out. For some items, such as buttons and controls, there is an audio description of the item.

NEW

There is also a Braille option that can be accessed at the bottom of the Narrator window. This has to be used in conjunction with third party software that communicates with a Braille display. This is a new feature in the Windows 10 Creators Update.

 Select options in the left-hand panel

Ease of Access

⌨ Narrator

🔍 Magnifier

☀ High contrast

CC Closed captions

⌨ Keyboard

🖱 Mouse

⟳ Other options

Each option has settings that can be applied. For instance, drag the **Narrator** button from **Off** to **On** to enable items to be read out on the screen

Narrator

Hear text and controls on the screen

Narrator is a screen reader that reads all the elements on screen, like text and buttons.

Narrator

⬤ Off

Start Narrator automatically

⬤ Off

4 Select **Magnifier** in Step 1, and turn Magnifier to **On** to activate the magnifying glass. Move this over areas of the screen to magnify them

5 Select the **High contrast** option in Step 1 and click in the **Choose a theme** box to select a color theme for text and background, for users who find it difficult reading black text on a white background

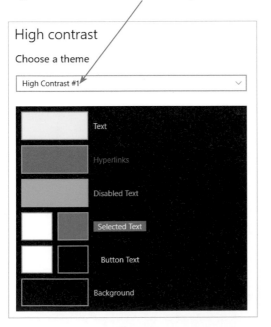

Date and Time Functions

To change the format Windows uses to display dates and times:

1 Select the **Settings** > **Time & language** option

Time & language
Speech, region, date

2 Click on the **Date & time** button

Date & time

Don't forget

If the **Set time automatically** button is **Off**, click on the **Change** button below **Change date and time** to set a manual date and time.

3 Drag the **Set time automatically** button to **On** to enable the computer to set the time and date

Date & time

Date and time

1:54 PM, Saturday, April 22, 2017

Set time automatically

On

Set time zone automatically

Off

Change date and time

Change

Time zone

(UTC+00:00) Dublin, Edinburgh, Lisbon, London

Adjust for daylight saving time automatically

On

4 Click on the **Region & language** button to set the default geographical region and language for the computer

Region & language

Region & language

Country or region

Windows and apps might use your country or region to give you local content

United States

Languages

You can type in any language you add to the list. Windows, apps and websites will appear in the first language in the list that they support

+ Add a language

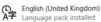 English (United States)
Windows display language

English (United Kingdom)
Language pack installed

6 File Explorer

The File Explorer is at the heart of working with the files on your computer, and you can use it to browse all of the information on your computer and on the local network. This chapter shows how you can use the Scenic Ribbon function, modify the views in File Explorer, use the Quick access folder, sort the contents, and customize the style and appearance.

Opening File Explorer

Although File Explorer (formerly called Windows Explorer) is not necessarily one of the first apps that you will use with Windows 10, it still plays an important role in organizing your folders and files. To access File Explorer:

 From the Desktop, click on this icon on the Taskbar, or

 Press **WinKey** + **E**, and File Explorer opens at the **Quick access** folder

 When File Explorer is opened, click on the **This PC** option to view the top level items on your computer, including the main folders, your hard drive and any removable devices that are connected

This PC displays files from different locations as a single collection, without actually moving any files.

You can click on the **Start** button and access File Explorer from here too.

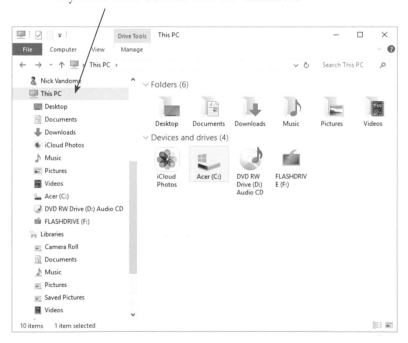

The Taskbar

The Taskbar is visible at the bottom of the screen and displays thumbnails of the apps that have been added there. To illustrate the range of functions that it supports:

1 Open items are displayed on the Taskbar at the bottom of the window (denoted by a white line underneath the item's icon)

File Explorer (also known as Explorer) is the program Explorer.exe. It handles the file system and user interfaces, and is sometimes referred to as the Windows Shell.

2 Right-click an open item on the Taskbar to view open files within the items and also recently viewed pages within it

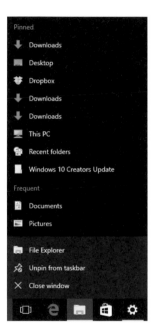

3 Move the mouse pointer over the File Explorer icon to see previews of the open folder windows that File Explorer is managing (if File Explorer is open)

Libraries

File Explorer can use the Library for accessing the files and folders on your computer and network. Each Library displays files from several locations. Initially, there are five Libraries defined:

● **Camera Roll**, which is the default folder for photos captured on your computer (if it has a camera attached).

● **Documents**, which is the default folder for files such as those created with word processing or presentation apps.

● **Music**, which is the default folder for music bought from the online Windows Store, or added yourself.

● **Pictures**, which is the default folder for your photos.

● **Videos**, which is the default folder for your videos.

To view the Pictures library, for example:

 Select **Libraries > Pictures** in the Navigation pane

To add another folder to the Pictures library:

 Right-click in the Pictures library window and select **New > Folder**

2 Click on the folder name and overwrite it with a new title

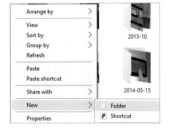

Beware

In Windows 10 the Libraries are not visible by default. To show them, click on the View button on the Scenic Ribbon, click on the **Navigation pane** button and click on the **Show libraries** button so that a tick appears.

Hot tip

You can also right-click the folder name in the Navigation pane folder list, to display the **New > Folder** menu.

124

Scenic Ribbon

The navigation and functionality in the Libraries is provided by the Scenic Ribbon at the top of the window. This has options for the Library itself and also the type of content that is being viewed.

1 Click on the tabs at the top of the Library window to view associated tools

2 Click on the Library Tools tab to view the menus for the whole Library (see below)

3 Click on the content tab (Picture Tools in this example) to view menus for the selected content

Library File menu
This contains options for opening a new window, closing the current window or moving to a frequently-visited location in the Library.

Library Home menu
This contains options for copying and pasting, moving, deleting and renaming selected items. You can also create new folders, view folder properties and select all items in a folder.

Don't forget

The Scenic Ribbon is also referred to as just the Ribbon.

125

Don't forget

The **File** button in the Ribbon remains highlighted in blue, regardless of which other menu is accessed.

...cont'd

Library Share menu

This contains options for sharing selected items, by sending them to the HomeGroup or another user on the computer, burning them to a CD or DVD, creating a compressed Zip file or sending the items to a printer.

Library View menu

This contains options for how you view the items in the current active folder (see page 136).

Click on the **Options** button on the View menu to set additional options for the operation of a folder and how items are displayed within it.

Library Manage menu

This contains options for managing specific libraries. Click on the **Manage library** button to add additional folders to the one currently being viewed.

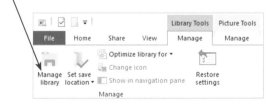

Library menu options

If there is a down-pointing arrow next to an item on a Library menu, click it to see additional options, such as the **Optimize library for** button, which optimizes the folder for specific types of content.

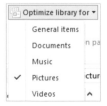

This PC Folder

One of the best ways to look at the contents of your computer involves using the This PC folder. To open this:

 1 Open File Explorer and select **This PC** in the Navigation pane

Navigation pane   Location   Search box

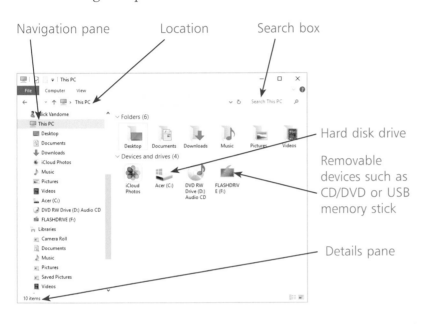

Hard disk drive

Removable devices such as CD/DVD or USB memory stick

Details pane

The Navigation pane provides the facilities you require to move between folders and drives.

2 Select items and double-click to view their contents

Quick Access

When working with files and folders there will probably be items which you access on a regular basis. The Quick access section of the File Explorer can be used to view the items that you have most recently accessed, and also to pin your most frequently used and favorite items. To use the Quick access section:

1 Click on the **Quick access** button in the File Explorer Navigation pane so that the right-pointing arrow becomes downwards-pointing

> ★ Quick access

∨ ★ Quick access

2 In the main window, your frequently used folders and most recently used files are displayed

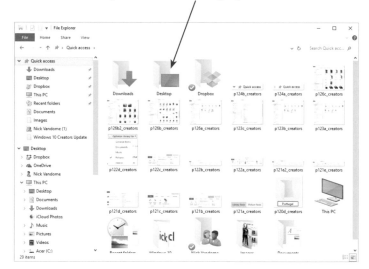

The items displayed under Quick access are not physically located here; the links are just shortcuts to the actual location within your file structure.

3 The folders are also listed underneath the **Quick access** button in the Navigation pane

∨ ★ Quick access
  ⬇ Downloads   📌
  🖥 Desktop   📌
  🗁 Dropbox   📌
  🖥 This PC   📌
  🗐 Recent folders   📌
  📄 Documents
  🖼 Images

Adding items to Quick access

The folders that you access and use most frequently can be pinned to the Quick access section. This does not physically move them; it just creates a shortcut within Quick access. To do this:

1 Right-click on the folder you want to pin, and click on **Pin to Quick access**

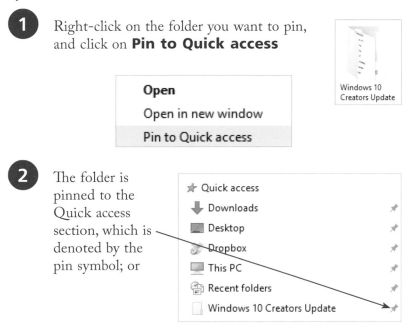

2 The folder is pinned to the Quick access section, which is denoted by the pin symbol; or

3 Drag the folder over the Quick access button until the **Pin to Quick access** option appears, and release

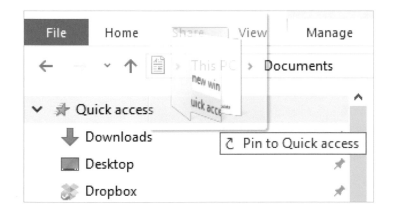

To unpin an item from Quick access, right-click on it and click on **Unpin from Quick access**.

129

Exploring Drives

Explore the contents of any drive from the This PC folder:

1 Select one of the drive icons – for example, the **Flashdrive** removable storage device

2 Double-click the **Flashdrive** device icon (or select it and press **Enter**) to display the files and folders that it contains

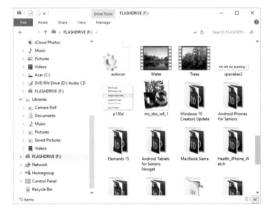

3 Double-click a folder entry (e.g. Windows 10 Creators Update) and select one of the files that it contains

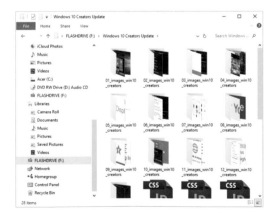

Press the **Back arrow** to go to the previous library or location, or click the **Down arrow** to select from the list of viewed locations. Click the **Up arrow** to move up one level.

4 Double-click the file icon and press **Enter** to open the file using the associated application

130

...cont'd

You can see all the folder entries in This PC in a structured list:

1 Double-click the **This PC** entry in the Navigation pane

2 The computer's folders are displayed, and the fixed drives plus any removable drives

with media inserted are listed

You can also explore the folders in Quick access, Libraries, HomeGroup and Network of attached computers.

3 Select the ❯ right-pointing arrow next to a heading level, to expand that entry to the next level

Resize the Navigation pane horizontally using the Stretch arrow, and traverse folder lists using the vertical scroll bar.

4 Select the ❯ down-pointing arrow to collapse the entries to that heading level

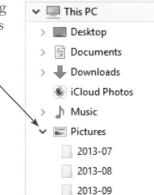

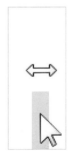

131

Address Bar

The Address bar at the top of File Explorer displays the current location as a set of names separated by arrows, and offers another way to navigate between libraries and locations.

1 To go to a location that is named in the address, click on that name in the Address bar, e.g. Documents

2 To select a subfolder of a library or location named in the Address bar, click on the arrow to the right

3 Click one of the entries to open it in place of the current location

When you are viewing a drive rather than a library, the Address bar shows the drive and its folders, and allows you to navigate amongst these.

You can specify a new location using the Address bar:

 Click on the Address bar in the blank space to the right of the set of names, and the full path is displayed

 Type the complete folder path, e.g. C:\Users\Public (or click in the path and amend the values), then press Enter

Hot tip

The path is highlighted, so typing a new path will completely replace the original values.

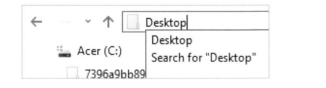 The specified location will be displayed

If you want a common location such as Desktop, just type the name alone and press **Enter**, and the location will be displayed:

Hot tip

You can switch to exploring the internet, by typing a web page address. The Microsoft Edge browser will be launched in a separate window.

Navigation Panes

The normal view for File Explorer includes the Navigation pane. There is also a Preview pane and a Details pane available.

You can choose different panes to display:

1 Open File Explorer and click on the **View** tab. This will open the Ribbon

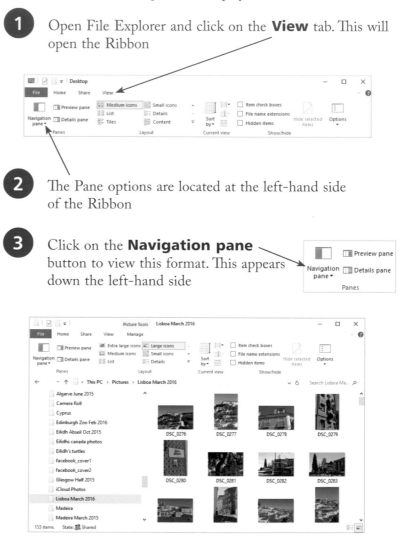

2 The Pane options are located at the left-hand side of the Ribbon

3 Click on the **Navigation pane** button to view this format. This appears down the left-hand side

If you check **Off** the Navigation pane in Step 4, the left-hand panel will not be visible in File Explorer.

4 Click on the arrow on the **Navigation pane** button and click here to show or hide the Navigation pane. There are also options here for showing or hiding the libraries

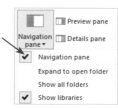

5 Click on the **Preview pane** button to view a preview of the folder or file selected in the main window

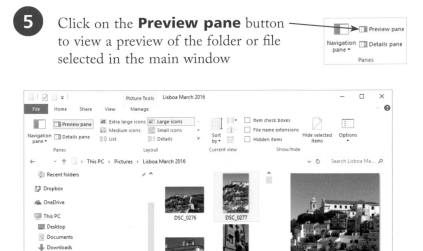

> **Don't forget**
>
> The Preview pane is particularly useful if you are working in the Pictures library.

6 Click on the **Details pane** button to view additional information about the folder or file selected in the main window

Changing Views

You can change the size and appearance of the file and folder icons in your folders, using the View tab on the Ribbon.

1 Open the folder you would like to change and click on the **View** tab on the Ribbon. Select one of the options for viewing content in the folder

View	Manage
▦ Extra large icons	▤ Large icons
▦ Medium icons	▦ Small icons
▦ List	▦ Details

Layout

Don't forget

The way items are displayed within folders can also be set within Folder Options (see page 140).

2 Click on different items to change the appearance of icons, such as from the Layout section

3 Hover the cursor over each **View** setting to preview. Click the mouse button to apply that view

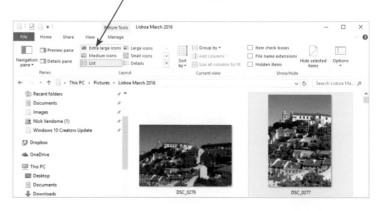

Sorting

Windows 10 allows you to sort your files in the drive or folder by various attributes or descriptors.

1 Open the folder, click on **View** > **Details** and select the attribute header that you want to sort by, e.g. Date

2 The entries are sorted into ascending order by the selected attribute. The header is shaded and a sort symbol ∧ added

Don't forget

Right-click on a column heading in Steps 2 and 3 to select which column headings appear, e.g. Date, Size, Type, etc.

3 Select the header again. The order is reversed and the header now shows an inverted sort symbol ∨

Hot tip

Note that any subfolders within your folder will be sorted to the end of the list when you reverse the sequence. Libraries are an exception, and keep folders at the top (in the appropriate sort order).

4 The contents will remain sorted in the selected sequence, even if you switch to a different folder view

Filtering

1 In the Details view (see page 136), select any header and click the **Down arrow** to the right-hand side

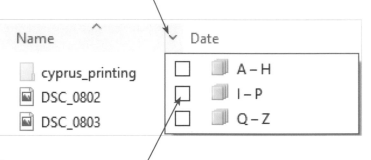

Hot tip

This shows ranges of values appropriate to the particular attribute, and based on the actual contents of the folder. These ranges are used for filtering and for grouping the items in the folder.

2 Select a box next to one or more ranges, and the items displayed are immediately restricted to that selection

3 You can select a second header, Size for example, to apply additional filtering to the items displayed

Hot tip

Filtering can only be applied in the **Details** folder view.

4 The tick ✓ symbol on headers indicates that filtering is in effect, and the Address bar shows the attributes

> This PC > Pictures > Cyprus > Large (1 - 16 MB)   ✓ ⟳   Search Cyprus

📌 ^   Date   Type   Size ✓ Tags

Beware

If you navigate away from the folder or close File Explorer, the next time you visit the folder, the filtering will have been removed.

5 Filtering remains in effect even if you change folder views within the selected folder

Grouping

You can group the contents of a folder using the header ranges.
You do not need to select the Details view.

 1 Right-click an empty part of the folder area, select **Group by**, then select an attribute, e.g. **Size**

The right-click context menu also offers the **Sort by** option, so you can specify or change the sort sequence without switching to Details view.

2 The contents will be grouped, using the ranges for the attribute selected

Any sorting that was already in place will remain in effect. However, you can switch between **Ascending** and **Descending**.

 3 Grouping is retained when you switch views (and when you revisit the folder after closing File Explorer)

Select **Group by** > **(None)** to remove grouping. Select **More...** to add other attributes. The new attributes will also appear in Details view.

4 You can regroup the folder contents by selecting another attribute. This will replace your original choice

Folder Options

You can change the appearance and the behavior of your folders by adjusting the folder settings.

 From the View tab on the Ribbon, click on the **Options** button and select the **Change folder and search options** link

The same dialog box is displayed if you access the **Control Panel** > **Appearance and Personalization** (from the Category view), then select **File Explorer Options**.

 Choose **Open each folder in its own window**, to keep multiple folders open at the same time

Folder Options ×

General View Search

Open File Explorer to: Quick access ⌄

Browse folders
○ Open each folder in the same window
◉ Open each folder in its own window

Click items as follows
○ Single-click to open an item (point to select)
   Underline icon titles consistent with my browser
   Underline icon titles only when I point at them
◉ Double-click to open an item (single-click to select)

Privacy
☑ Show recently used files in Quick access
☑ Show frequently used folders in Quick access
Clear File Explorer history   [Clear]

[Restore Defaults]

[OK]   [Cancel]   [Apply]

140

To open a subfolder in its own window, when **Open each folder in the same window** is set, right-click the subfolder and select **Open in new window**.

If you want items to open as they do on a web page, select **Single-click to open an item (point to select)**

Select the **View** tab to select options for how items appear in the File Explorer libraries

Select **Apply** to try out the selected changes without closing the Folder Options, then **OK** to confirm

[Apply]

Alternatively, select **Restore Defaults** then **Apply**, to reset all options to their default values

[Restore Defaults]

7 Managing Files and Folders

Folders can contain other folders as well as files, and Windows 10 treats them in very much the same way. Hence, operations such as moving, copying, deleting and searching apply to files and to folders in a similar way. This chapter shows how to perform these tasks while working with File Explorer.

Select Files and Folders

To process several files or folders, it is more efficient to select and process them as a group, rather than one by one:

Single file or folder

 Click the item to highlight it, then move, copy or delete it as required

Sequential files

Use the sorting, filtering and grouping options (see pages 137-139) to rearrange the files to make the selection easier.

 To highlight a range, click to select the first item, press and hold **Shift**, then click the last item

Adjacent block

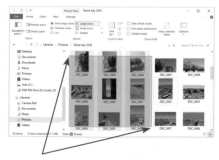

You must start the selection box from an empty space in the folder. If you accidentally click a file or folder, you will drag that item, rather than create a box.

 Click and hold, then drag out a box to cover the files you want selected. All the files in the rectangular area will be highlighted

Non-adjacent files

 To select several non-adjacent files, click one item, press and hold **Ctrl**, then click the subsequent items. As you select files, they are highlighted

Partial sequence
You can combine these techniques to select part of a range.

 Select a group of sequential files or an adjacent block of files (as described on the previous page)

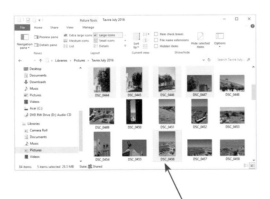

Hot tip

To deselect one file, click it while the **Ctrl** key is being held down. To deselect all of the files, click once anywhere in the folder outside of the selection area.

2 Hold down **Ctrl** and click to deselect any files in the range that you do not want, and to select extra ones

All files and folders
To select all of the files (and folders) in the current folder, select the **Home** tab on the Ribbon and click on **Select All** or press **Ctrl** + **A**.

Beware

If you select a folder, you will also be selecting any files and folders that it may contain.

Copy or Move Files or Folders

You may wish to copy or move files and folders to another folder on the same drive, or to another drive. There are several ways to achieve this:

Drag, using the right mouse button

Hot tip

For ease and simplicity, the prompted method using the right mouse button is recommended.

 Open File Explorer and the folder with the required files, then locate the destination in the Folders list in the Navigation pane

 In the folder contents, select the files and folders that you want to copy or move

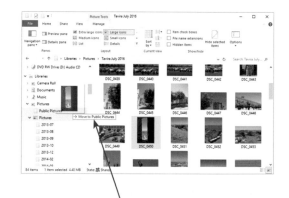

 Right-click any one of the selection, drag the files onto the destination folder or drive in the Folders list, so it is highlighted and named, then release to display the menu

 Click the **Move here** or **Copy here** option as desired, and the files will be added to the destination folder

Copy here
Move here
Create shortcuts here
Cancel

Drag, using the left mouse button

In this case, default actions are applied with no intervening menu.

 Select the files and folders to be moved or copied

Hot tip

Open File Explorer and the source folder, then locate the destination in the Folders list in the Navigation pane, ready for moving or copying files and folders.

 Use the left mouse button to drag the selection to the destination drive or folder in the Folders list – in this example, the removable USB storage drive (Flashdrive)

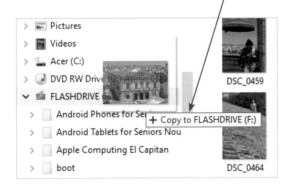

Hot tip

As you hover over a drive or folder in the Folders list in the Navigation pane, it expands to reveal the subfolders.

3 Press **Shift** to Move instead of Copy to another drive. Press **Ctrl** to Copy instead of Move to a folder on the same drive as the source folder

Don't forget

You will see a ✚ symbol if the file is going to be copied, or a ➜ if the file is going to be moved.

In summary

Drives	Drag	Drag + Shift	Drag + Ctrl
Same	Move	Move	Copy
Different	Copy	Move	Copy

...cont'd

Using Cut, Copy and Paste

Cut does not remove the selection initially, it just dims it until you Paste it (see Step 5). Press **Esc** if you decide to cancel the move, and the item will remain in place.

 Choose the files and folders you want to copy, and right-click within the selection

 From the context menu, click **Copy** or **Cut** to move the selection

3 Move to the destination folder (or create a new one)

4 Right-click a blank area of the destination folder

5 Select **Paste** from the menu to complete the Copy or move operation

When you Copy, you can **Paste shortcut** (instead of Paste) to insert a link to the original file. However, this is inactive when you Cut files.

Keyboard shortcuts

Cut, Copy and Paste options are also available as keyboard shortcuts. Select files and folders as above, but use these keys in place of the menu selections for Copy, Cut and Paste. There are also shortcuts to Undo an action or Redo an action.

Press this key	To do this
F1	Display Help
Ctrl+C	Copy the selected item
Ctrl+X	Cut the selected item
Ctrl+V	Paste the selected item
Ctrl+Z	Undo an action
Ctrl+Y	Redo an action

...cont'd

Burn to disc

If your computer has a CD or DVD recorder, you can copy files to a writable disc. This is usually termed "burning".

1 Insert a writable CD or DVD disc into the recorder drive (DVD/CD RW). Click on this pop-up

DVD RW Drive (D:)
Tap to choose what happens with removable drives.

2 When the prompt appears, choose the option to **Burn files to disc** using File Explorer

DVD RW Drive (D:)

Choose what to do with blank DVDs.

Burn files to disc
File Explorer

Take no action

3 Make sure the CD/DVD is selected, and copy and paste files into the main window, drag files there to copy them to the disc, or

Drive Tools — DVD RW Drive (D:)

File   Home   Share   View   Manage

← → ↑ ◯ › This PC › DVD RW Drive (D:) ›   ✓ ↻   Search DVD RW D... 🔎

Files Ready to Be Written to the Disc (1)

Windows 10

1 item

Don't forget

You can use any of the methods described for copying or moving one or more files and folders (see pages 144-146).

4 Select files within another File Explorer window and click on the **Burn to disc** button under the **Share** tab

File   Home   Share   View

Share   Email   Zip

🔥 Burn to disc
🖨 Print
📠 Fax

File Conflicts

When you copy or move files from one folder to another, conflicts may arise. There may already be a file with the same name in the destination folder. To illustrate what may happen:

 Open a folder, e.g. **Documents > Windows 10 Creators Update** folder and the USB Flashdrive

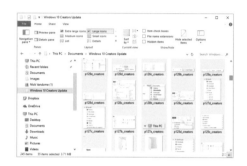

 Press **Ctrl** + **A** to select all of the files and drag them onto the Flashdrive, to initiate a copy of them

 Windows observes a conflict – some files already exist, with identical size and date information. Select one of the options

Hot tip

You can, of course, use the Copy and Paste options from the right-click menus, or use the equivalent keyboard shortcuts, and File Explorer will continue to check for possible conflicts.

4 If you select the **Let me decide for each file** option, details will be displayed so you can view if one is newer than another. Click on the **Continue** button to confirm the decisions made

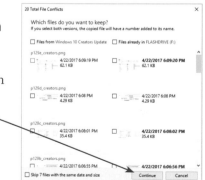

Open Files

You can open a file using an associated app without first having to explicitly start that app. There are several ways to do this:

Default program

1 Double-click the file icon, or

2 Right-click the file and select **Open** from the menu, or

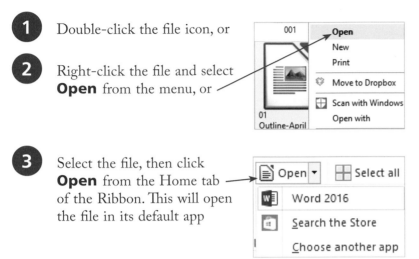

Default programs can also be set in **Control Panel** > **Programs** > **Default programs** (in Category view).

3 Select the file, then click **Open** from the Home tab of the Ribbon. This will open the file in its default app

Alternative program (app)

You may have several apps that can open a particular file type. To use a different app than the default to open the file:

1 Right-click the file icon and select **Open with**. Pick an app from the list or click **Choose another app** to set a new default app

2 The same choices are presented when you select the Down arrow next to the **Open** button on the Ribbon in the folder window

Delete Files and Folders

When you want to remove files or folders, you use the same delete procedures – whatever drive or device the items are stored on.

 Choose one or more files and folders, selected as described previously (see pages 142-143)

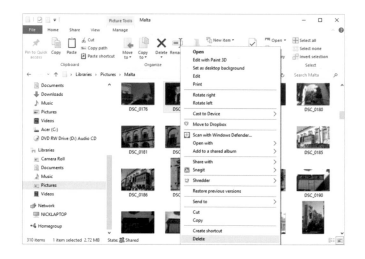

Right-click the selection and click **Delete**

Alternatively, click on the **Delete** button on the Ribbon, or click the arrow and select one of the options

If you choose to delete and then immediately realize that you have made a mistake deleting one or more files, right-click the folder area and select **Undo Delete** or press **Ctrl** + **Z**, to reverse the last operation. For hard disk items, you are also able to retrieve deleted files from the Recycle Bin, and this could be a substantial time later (unless you have emptied or bypassed the Recycle Bin – see pages 152-153).

The Recycle Bin

The Recycle Bin is, in effect, a folder on your hard disk that holds deleted files and folders. They are not physically removed from your hard disk (unless you empty the Recycle Bin or delete specific items from within the Recycle Bin itself). They will remain there until the Recycle Bin fills up, at which time the oldest deleted files may finally be removed.

The Recycle Bin, therefore, provides a safety net for files and folders you may delete by mistake, and allows you to easily retrieve them, even at a later date.

Restoring files

1 Double-click on the **Recycle Bin** icon from the Desktop or in the Navigation pane

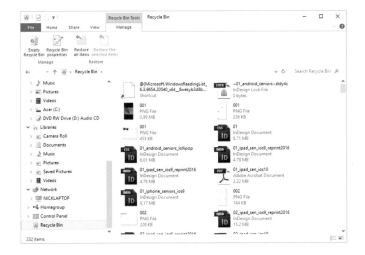

2 Select the **Restore all items** button, or select a file and the button changes to **Restore this item**

To see where the Recycle Bin is located, right-click in a clear area of the **Navigation pane** and select **Show all folders**.

| ✓ Show libraries |
| ✓ Show all folders |
| Expand to current folder |

A restored folder will include all the files and subfolders that it held when it was originally deleted.

...cont'd

Permanently erase files

You may want to explicitly delete particular files, perhaps for reasons of privacy and confidentiality.

 Open the Recycle Bin

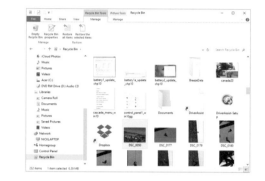

Don't forget

You do not have to worry about the space used in the Recycle Bin. Windows keeps track and removes the oldest deleted entries when the maximum allowed space, typically 10% of the drive, has been used.

 Select the relevant files and folders, then select **Delete** from the one of the menus (or press the **Delete** key)

 Select **Yes**, to confirm that you want to permanently delete these files (completely remove them from the hard disk)

Empty the Recycle Bin

If desired, you can remove all of the contents of the Recycle Bin from the hard disk:

 With the Recycle Bin open, select the **Empty Recycle Bin** button

 Press **Yes** to confirm the permanent deletion

The Recycle Bin icon changes from full to empty, to illustrate the change.

Hot tip

Right-click the Recycle Bin icon and select **Empty Recycle Bin**, to remove all of the files and folders without it being open.

Expand
Open in new window
Empty Recycle Bin
Pin to Start
Rename
Properties

Bypass the Recycle Bin

If you want to prevent particular deleted files from being stored in the Recycle Bin:

1 From their original location, select the files and folders, right-click the selection, but this time hold down the **Shift** key as you select **Delete**

Cut
Copy

Create shortcut
Delete
Rename

2 Confirm that you want to permanently delete the selected item or items. "Permanent" means that no copy will be kept

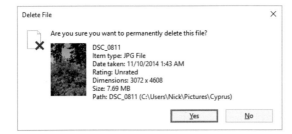

Delete File   ×

Are you sure you want to permanently delete this file?

DSC_0811
Item type: JPG File
Date taken: 11/10/2014 1:43 AM
Rating: Unrated
Dimensions: 3072 x 4608
Size: 7.69 MB
Path: DSC_0811 (C:\Users\Nick\Pictures\Cyprus)

Yes   No

Hot tip

You could also just press the **Delete** key on the keyboard to delete items, or **Shift** + the **Delete** key to delete items permanently.

153

Deactivate (or resize) the Recycle Bin

You can tell Windows to always bypass the Recycle Bin:

1 Right-click the Recycle Bin icon, then select **Properties** from the menu

Expand

Open in new window
Empty Recycle Bin
Pin to Start

Rename

Properties

2 Note the space available in the Recycle Bin location (free space on hard disk)

3 Adjust the maximum size allowed, to resize the Recycle Bin

General

Recycle Bin Location   Space Available
Acer (C:)   678 GB

Settings for selected location
○ Custom size:
    Maximum size (MB):   36804
◉ Don't move files to the Recycle Bin. Remove files
   immediately when deleted.

☐ Display delete confirmation dialog

4 Click the button labeled **Don't move files to the Recycle Bin. Remove files immediately when deleted**, to always bypass the Recycle Bin

Beware

Take extra care when selecting files and folders if you are bypassing the Recycle Bin, since you will have no recovery options.

Create a Folder

You can create a new folder in a drive, folder or on the Desktop:

Make sure that you click in the space between icons, away from the (usually hidden) boxes surrounding the icons.

1 Right-click an empty part of the folder window, select **New** and then **Folder**

2 Overtype the default name New Folder, e.g. type *Articles*, and press **Enter**

If you click away from the icon without typing the new name, you get folders called New Folder, New Folder (2), and so on.

You can also create a new file in a standard format for use with one of the apps installed on your computer:

1 Right-click an empty part of the folder, select **New**, and choose the specific file type, e.g. Text Document file

Normally, the file name extension (which shows the file type) will be hidden. To reveal file extensions, open **Folder Options**, select the **View** tab and clear the box labeled **Hide extensions for known file types**.

2 Overtype the file name provided, and press **Enter**

Rename a File or Folder

You can rename a file or folder at any time, by simply editing the current name:

 1 Right-click the file/folder, then click **Rename**, or select the icon and click on the icon name

Hot tip

Use the same method to rename icons on the Desktop. You can even rename the Recycle Bin.

2 Either way, the current name will be highlighted. Type a name to delete and replace the current name, or press the arrow keys to position the typing cursor and edit the existing name:

Don't forget

You must always provide a non-blank file name, and you should avoid special characters such as quote marks, question marks and periods.

3 Press **Enter** or click elsewhere to confirm the new name

Preserving file types

When you have file extensions revealed and you create or rename a file or folder, only the name itself, not the file type, will be highlighted. This avoids accidental changes of type.

Beware

You can change the file type (extension), but you will be warned that this may make the file unusable.

Backtrack File Operations

If you accidentally delete, rename, copy or move the wrong file or folder, you can undo (reverse) the last operation and preceding operations, to get back to where you started. For example:

Hot tip

Undo mistakes as soon as possible since you would have to undo subsequent operations first. Also, only a limited amount of undo history is maintained.

Don't forget

The Undo command that is offered changes depending on which operation was being performed at the time.

Don't forget

If you go back too far, right-click the folder and select the available Redo operation, e.g. Redo Rename.

Beware

Undo commands do not work on permanently deleted files.

 Right-click the folder area and select the **Undo Rename** command that is displayed

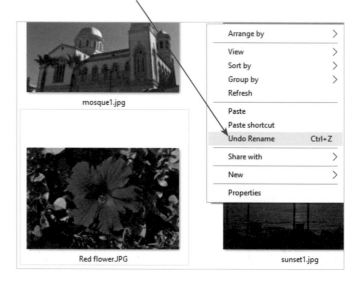

Right-click again, and this time there is an **Undo Delete** command for you to select

Now you will have reversed the last two operations, putting the folder and files back as they were before the changes

File Properties

Every file (and every folder) has information that can be displayed in the Properties dialog box. To display this:

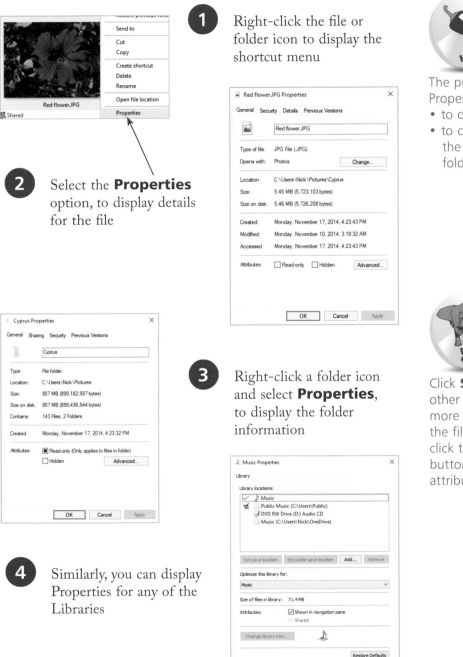

1 Right-click the file or folder icon to display the shortcut menu

2 Select the **Properties** option, to display details for the file

3 Right-click a folder icon and select **Properties**, to display the folder information

4 Similarly, you can display Properties for any of the Libraries

Hot tip

The purpose of the Properties dialog box is:
• to display details
• to change settings for the selected file or folder.

Don't forget

Click **Security** and the other tabs, to display more information about the file or folder, and click the **Advanced...** button for additional attributes.

Search for Files and Folders

If you are not quite sure where exactly you stored a file, or what the full name is, the File Explorer Search box may be the answer.

Hot tip

Open the library or folder that is most likely to hold the file you want, then click in the Search box to initiate a search, looking at file names and content limited to that folder and its subfolders.

 Open a location, e.g. Documents, click in the Search box and start typing a word from the file, e.g. *Nick*

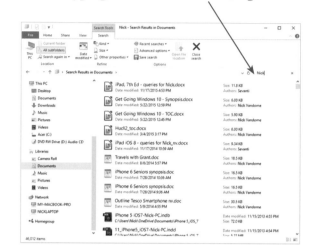

Don't forget

Some files contain the search words in the file names, while others contain the words within the textual content.

 If that produces too many files, start typing another word that might help limit the number of matches, e.g. *Vandome*

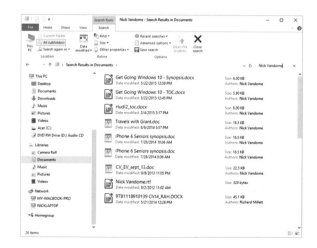

Hot tip

For an attached hard drive, you may be offered the option to **Click to add to index**, and thereby speed up future searches. Indexing is the process of the Search facility storing the words that can be searched over.

Hot tip

You can also use Cortana to search for files and folders (see pages 57-59).

 If the location is a drive rather than a library, its contents may not be indexed, so the search may take longer

Compressed Folders

This feature allows you to save disk space by compressing files and folders, while allowing them to be treated as normal by Windows 10.

Create a compressed folder

 1 Right-click an empty portion of the folder window and select **New** > **Compressed (zipped) Folder**

Hot tip

Compressed folders are distinguished from other folders by a zipper on the folder icon. They are compatible with other zip archive apps, such as WinZip.

2 A compressed folder is created, with the default name New Compressed (zipped) Folder.zip

3 Rename it (see page 155). You can also open, move, or delete it just like any other folder

New Compressed (zipped) Folder.zip

159

Don't forget

To create a compressed folder and copy a file into it at the same time: right-click a file in File Explorer, select **Send to** > **Compressed (zipped) folder**. The new compressed folder has the same file name, but with a file extension of .zip.

Add files or folders to a compressed folder

1 Drag files or folders onto a compressed folder and they will automatically be compressed and stored there

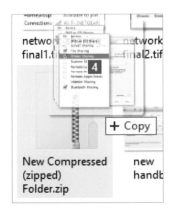

+ Copy

New Compressed (zipped) Folder.zip

...cont'd

Compressed item Properties

 Double-click the compressed folder and select any file to see the compressed size versus the original size

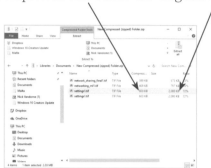

Right-click the file and select **Properties** to display this information, if the Details panel has not been enabled (see page 136).

Extract files and folders

 Open the compressed folder, drag files and folders onto a normal folder and they will be decompressed. The compressed version still remains in the compressed folder, unless you hold the Shift key as you drag (i.e. Move)

Extract all

 To extract all of the files and folders from a compressed folder, right-click it and then click on **Extract all** or select it from the Extract section on the Ribbon

Extract all

 Accept or edit the target folder and click **Extract**. The files and folders are decompressed and transferred

If the folder specified does not exist, it will be created automatically.

8 Digital Lifestyle

Windows 10 covers a range of entertainment with the Photos, Groove Music and Movies & TV apps, and the new Paint 3D app for creating 3D items. This chapter shows how to work with these apps and also the online OneDrive function for backing up content.

Using OneDrive

Cloud computing is now a mainstream part of our online experience. This involves saving content to an online server connected to the service that you are using, i.e. through your Microsoft Account. You can then access this content from any computer, using your account login details, and also share it with other people by giving them access to your Cloud service. It can also be used to back up your files, in case they get corrupted or damaged on your PC.

The Cloud service with Windows 10 is known as OneDrive, and you can use it providing that you have a Microsoft Account.

Click on these buttons on the right-hand side of the OneDrive toolbar in Step 3 to, from left to right: sort the content; display it with its details; as thumbnails; or with the details pane.

1 Click on the **OneDrive** app on the Start Menu and follow the wizard to sign in to OneDrive

2 Open File Explorer and click on the **OneDrive** folder to view its contents

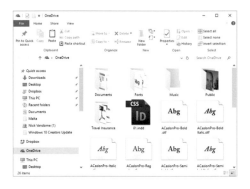

3 To view the contents of OneDrive online, go to the website at **onedrive.live.com** and sign in with your Microsoft Account details. Your OneDrive content is the same as in your OneDrive folder on your computer. Click on items to open, view and edit them

Click on these buttons on the left-hand side of the OneDrive toolbar in Step 3 to, from left to right: create new folders in the file structure, and upload files from other locations.

OneDrive Settings

A range of settings can be applied to OneDrive, including adding
and syncing folders. To do this:

1 Right-click on the OneDrive icon on
the Notification area of the Taskbar
and click on **Settings**

View sync problems
Manage storage
Settings
Help ⟩
Exit

2 Click on the
Settings tab
for options
for starting
OneDrive when
you sign in, and
for unlinking
your OneDrive
so that it does
not sync with
the online
function

⚓ Microsoft OneDrive   ✕

Settings Account About

More info
Get help with OneDrive   Terms of use
Privacy & Cookies   Third party notices

About Microsoft OneDrive
Version 2016 (Build 17.3.6816.0313)
© 2016 Microsoft Corporation. All rights reserved.

[OK] [Cancel]

3 Click on the
Account tab
and click on
the **Choose
folders** button
to select the
folder from
your computer
that you want
to sync with
your OneDrive
account

⚓ Microsoft OneDrive   ✕

Settings Account Auto Save Network Office About

OneDrive (nickvandome@gmail.com)
2.9 GB of 5.0 GB cloud storage used   [Add an account]
Get more storage   Unlink this PC

Choose folders
Folders you choose will be available on this PC.   [Choose folders]

[OK] [Cancel]

4 Click on the **OK**
button to apply
any changes to the OneDrive settings

Adding Files to OneDrive

OneDrive is built into the file structure of Windows 10, and as well as adding files from OneDrive itself, it is also possible to add them to the OneDrive folder from your computer. Once this has been done, the files can be accessed from OneDrive from your computer, online, or any compatible device, using your Microsoft Account login details.

Adding from File Explorer

To add files from File Explorer:

Your OneDrive folder can be pinned to the Quick access section in File Explorer. To do this, right-click on the OneDrive icon in File Explorer and click on **Pin to Quick access**.

Hot tip

By default, you get 5GB of free OneDrive storage space with Windows 10 (the free allowance was reduced from 15GB in July 2016). This is an excellent way to back up your important documents, since they are stored away from your computer. For up-to-date information on plan allowances and pricing, visit **https:// onedrive.live.com/ about/plans/**

1 In File Explorer, the OneDrive folder is located underneath Quick access (and any other folders that have been added)

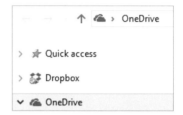

2 Click on the OneDrive folder to view its contents

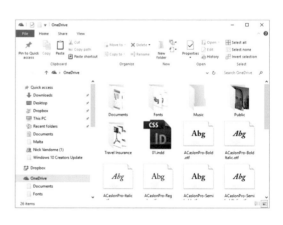

3 Add files to the OneDrive folder by dragging and dropping them from another folder or by using Copy and Paste

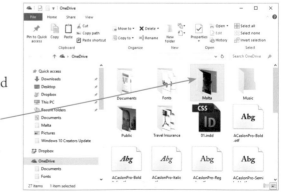

...cont'd

4 The new content is available from the OneDrive app and also online from your OneDrive account

Saving files to OneDrive

Files can also be saved directly to OneDrive when they are created. To do this:

1 Open a new file in any app, and create the required content

2 Select **File** > **Save** from the menu bar and select a OneDrive folder into which you want to save the file

3 Click on the **Save** button

4 The file is saved into the OneDrive folder and will be available from the OneDrive app, and also online from your OneDrive account

Hot tip

You can share your **Public** folder from your online OneDrive account by opening it and clicking or tapping on the **Share** button. You can then email the link to the Public folder to selected recipients.

165

Viewing Photos

The Photos app can be used to manage and edit your photos, including those stored in your **Pictures** Library. To do this:

 Click on the **Photos** app on the **Start Menu**

The **Photos** app interface has been updated in the Windows 10 Creators Update.

2 The main categories are at the left-hand side of the top toolbar

Collection   Albums   Folders   Bing

3 Other options are at the right-hand side of the toolbar, including refreshing the current item, selecting an item(s), playing the current photos in a slideshow and importing photos

Hot tip

To import photos into the Photos app, click on this button on the top toolbar

and select the location from where you want to import the photos. This can be a folder on your own computer; a camera or flashdrive attached with a USB cable; or a memory card from a camera inserted into a card reader.

4 Click on the **Collection** button to view all of the photos in the Photos app, arranged by date. Scroll up and down to view the photos

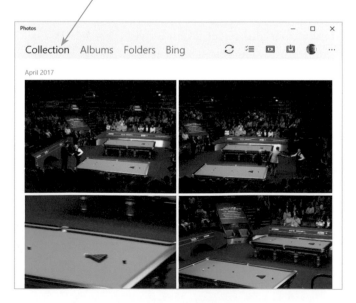

5 Click on the **Albums** button to view photos from specific albums. This includes the Camera Roll

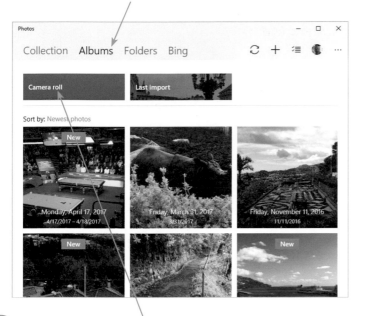

The albums displayed are taken from those stored in the specific folders in File Explorer (by default, the Pictures library). However, the Photos app displays what it thinks are the best photos in the folder, thus creating its own albums.

6 Click on the **Camera roll** album to view photos that have been taken with your computer's camera (or copied into this folder from another location)

...cont'd

Don't forget

Albums can include photos and videos.

7   Within the Albums section, double-click on an album to view its contents. The first photo is also displayed as a banner at the top of the album

8   Double-click on a photo within an album, or collection, to view it at full size. Move the cursor over the photo and click on the left and right arrows (if available) to move through an album or collection

9   Click here to view the photo in full screen mode

...cont'd

Sharing photos

Photos within either a collection or an album in the Photos app can be selected and then shared with other people in various ways, or deleted. To do this:

1 In Collections, or an open Album, click on the **Select** button on the top toolbar

2 Click here to select a photo or photos

3 Click on the **Share** button to share the selected photo(s)

4 Click on one of the options for sharing the selected photo(s)

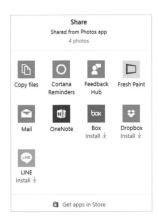

The **Share menu** has been updated throughout the Windows 10 Creators Update and has the same appearance as in Step 4.

5 Alternatively, click on the Copy button on the top toolbar, instead of the Share button in Step 3, to copy a selected image, so that it can then be pasted into another app

Editing Photos

In Windows 10 the Photos app has a range of editing functions so that you can improve and enhance your photos. To use these:

1 Open a photo at full size

2 Click on the **Edit** button on the top toolbar (or click on the **Menu** button first if the Edit button is not showing) to access additional editing options. Scroll up and down the right-hand panel to view the editing options

3 Click on the **Crop and rotate** button in Step 2 to crop the current photo or rotate it in a variety of ways, such as flipping horizontally or vertically or by a specific amount, by dragging here

Hot tip

Most photos benefit from some degree of cropping, so that the main subject is given greater prominence by removing unwanted items in the background.

4 Click on the **Enhance** button in Step 2 to apply filter effects. Click on the **Adjust** button to adjust elements in the photos by dragging on these bars for each element

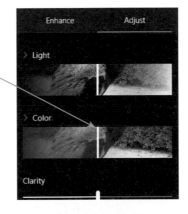

171

5 As the bar moves, so the elements of the photos are amended

6 Click here next to one of the editing functions to view additional items

7 Click on the **Save** button to save the changes to the original photo, or **Save a copy** to create a new image

Groove Music App

The Groove Music app is used to access music that you have added to your computer and also the Music section of the Windows Store, where you can preview, buy and download more music.

1 Click on the **Groove Music** app on the Start menu

2 Click on the Menu button to expand the menu so that the titles are visible, not just the icons

3 Click on a category to view those items

4 Click on the **Explore** button to access the Music section of the Windows Store

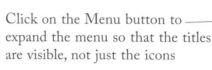

5 Browse through the Store using the categories in the main window. Click on an item to view details about it

6 Once you have selected an item, you can preview individual tracks, view information about the artist, and buy albums or specific tracks

Don't forget

Scroll up and down to view the rest of the available content in the Music section of the Windows Store.

Don't forget

Music that has been bought in the Music section of the Windows Store is then available to be played within the Groove Music app.

Playing Music

Playing your own music

Music that has been added to your computer can be played through the Groove Music app, and you can automatically specify new music to be included when it is added. To do this:

1 Open the Groove Music app and click on the **My music** button

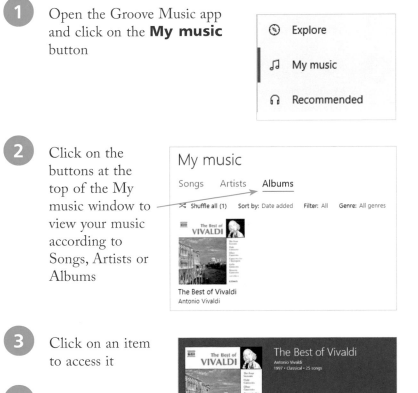

2 Click on the buttons at the top of the My music window to view your music according to Songs, Artists or Albums

3 Click on an item to access it

4 Click on a track or album to start playing it

5 Use these buttons above to, from left to right: go to the start of a track; pause/play a track; go to the end of a track; shuffle the available tracks; repeat a track; or change or mute the volume

You can also add music to the Groove Music app from the Library that you have stored in your OneDrive folder.

When a folder is added to the Music library, any music that is copied here will be displayed by the Groove Music app.

Do not copy music and use it for commercial purposes, as this will infringe the copyright of the artist.

Viewing Movies and TV

For movie and TV lovers, the Movies & TV app performs a similar function to the Groove Music app. It connects to the Windows Store from where you can preview and buy your favorite movies and TV shows.

Don't forget

The Movies & TV app is called **Films & TV** in some regions.

Don't forget

Movies and TV shows can be streamed (viewed from the computer server where the item is stored, rather than downloading it) if you have a fast internet connection. They can also be downloaded to a single device so that they can be viewed while you are offline.

1 Click on the **Movies & TV** app on the Start menu

2 The Windows Store opens at the Movies & TV section. Click on these buttons to view the items in the Movies & TV section and items you have bought

3 Click on the **Movies** (or **TV**) button to view the available items

4 Click on an item to see more information, view a preview clip, buy or rent and download the movie

Books in Windows 10

Windows 10 now caters for eBooks, which can be downloaded from the Windows Store and read on your Windows 10 device:

 1 Open the **Windows Store** and click on the **Books** button on the top toolbar

Books

 2 The range of books is displayed and can be navigated around in a similar way as for music or movies and TV

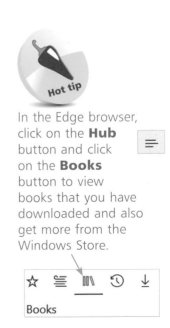

Books in the Windows Store is a new feature in the Windows 10 Creators Update.

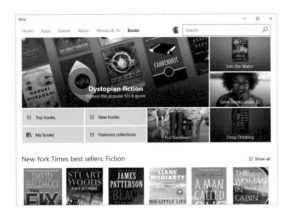

3 Tap on a book to see details about it. Tap on the **Buy** button to download the full text, or the **Preview** button to view a free sample

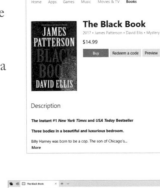

In the Edge browser, click on the **Hub** button and click on the **Books** button to view books that you have downloaded and also get more from the Windows Store.

 4 Books from the Windows Store are displayed within the Edge browser. Tap the space bar to move forwards through the pages, or click on the left- and right-hand sides of the screen to move in those directions

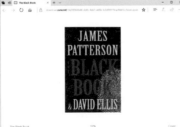

Using Paint 3D

The Windows 10 Creators Update caters for a wide range of 3D use, and one of the most significant is the Paint 3D app that can be used to create your own 3D pictures and also import ones from other places.

Around Paint 3D

Paint 3D is a new feature in the Windows 10 Creators Update.

In some ways, Paint 3D is an extension of the Windows Paint app. However, it has a much greater array of features, and brings the creation of 3D pictures within reach of anyone. To get started with creating 3D pictures:

1 Click on the **Paint 3D** app

2 The Home screen displays a range of options, including creating a new project, opening an existing one, pasting a copied 3D object, and introductory help videos

3 Click on the **New** button to create a new, blank, project

4 The Paint 3D workspace includes the canvas (the white square in the middle), the background, the tools for creating content, and the tools palette (at the right-hand side)

5 Click on this button at the top of the screen to display the Paint 3D toolbar

6 If the Paint 3D app is maximized, the workspace is expanded and the whole toolbar is permanently displayed at the top of the screen

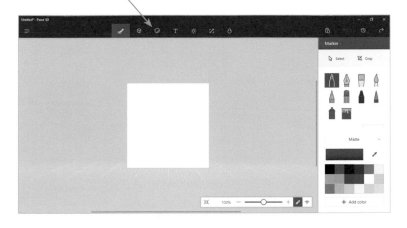

Hot tip

Click on these buttons on the top toolbar to, from left to right: select the canvas to manage its properties; access Remix 3D, which is an online facility for sharing 3D images with other online users and downloading those that other people have created. This is done within the Xbox Live environment.

7 Click on the button in Step 5 to select a drawing tool for creating standard 2D drawings

8 Click here to select a color for the drawing tool, or click on the **Add color** button to create a custom color for the tool

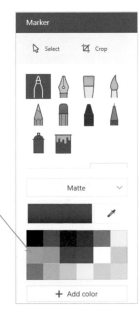

...cont'd

Adding 3D content

Paint 3D really comes into its own when you start adding and editing 3D shapes, stickers and text. To do this:

 Click on the **3D objects** button on the top toolbar

 Click on one of the 3D objects to select it. Select a color for it in the same way as for one of the drawing tools

3 Click on the canvas to add the object

4 Some objects appear initially as 2D shapes

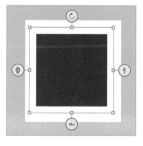

5 Use the controls around the object to move to display the 3D effect

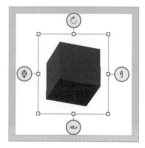

6 Drag on this button to zoom in and out on the canvas

7 Click on the **Stickers** button on the top toolbar

8 Click on this button, then click on one of the stickers to select it

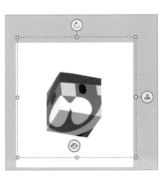

When one of the top toolbar options is selected, these buttons at the right-hand side of the window can be used to, from left to right: paste content that has been copied; undo actions; view the history of the actions performed on the current image (and rewind back through the editing process, if required); and redo actions that have been undone.

9 Click on an object on the canvas to add the sticker to it. The object will take on the properties of the sticker (the sticker can also be added on its own on the canvas, in which case it initially appears in 2D)

10 Click on the **Text** button on the top toolbar

11 Click on this button to create 3D text and make selections for the text below, including font, size, color, bold, italic, underlining and alignment

Stickers can be added directly to the canvas, in which case they appear as 2D objects, although they can be converted to 3D by clicking on the **Make 3D** button in the 3D objects editing panel.

...cont'd

Click on the Paint 3D
Menu button

to access options for
creating new images,
opening existing ones,
saving an image,
uploading an image to
Remix 3D, printing an
image or sharing it.

- 📄 New
- 📱 Open
- ↓ Insert
- 💾 Save
- 📝 Save as

- ↑ Upload to Remix 3D
- 🖶 Print
- ↪ Share

 Click on the canvas to
create a text box and type
the required text

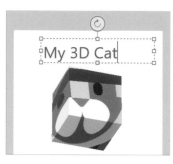

 Press **Enter** on the
keyboard to confirm
the text and activate the
rotation controls

 Drag on the rotation
controls to create the 3D
effect for the text

15 Click on the **Effects** button
on the top toolbar

16 Click on a background color for the
effect to be added to the image

 Click on the image to add
the effect. This is added to the
canvas and the background
behind it

Gaming with Windows 10

The gaming experience has been enhanced in theWindows 10 Creators Update, with an overhaul of the Xbox app interface, for playing games and interacting with other gamers. To play games with the Windows 10 Creators Update:

1 Click on the **Start** button and click on the **Xbox** app

2 Click on the **Home** button to view the Xbox Homepage. This contains the **Toolbar** (down the left-hand side), the **Activity feed** (in the

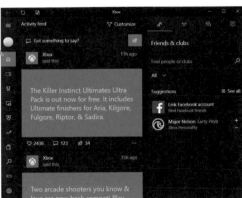

left-hand panel) and the options for joining clubs and connecting with other gamers (in the right-hand panel)

3 Click on the **My games** button to view system games or those that you have downloaded from the Windows Store

4 Click on the **Achievements** button to view your scores from games you have played, and compare them with other gamers

The Xbox app has been updated for the Windows 10 Creators Update.

You have to be signed in with your Microsoft Account in order to use the Xbox app and all of its features.

Click on the **Play** button next to a game in Step 3 to open it and start playing it.

...cont'd

5 Click on the **Clubs** button to view details of online game playing clubs. This is where you can join up with other players, to compare scores and also play online games against other players (multiplayer games)

6 In the right-hand panel, click on the **Friends list** button to view friends that you have added (this can be done by searching for them through the Xbox app in the **Find people of clubs** box, or by linking to them via Facebook)

7 Click on the **Parties** button to create a group of multiplayer gamers, who can all play together

8 Click on the **Messages** button to send messages to people in your groups and clubs, and also view messages you have received

9 Click on the **Activity alert** button to view any activity in relation to messages you have sent or comments you have made

9 Microsoft Edge Browser

The Microsoft Edge browser is fast and responsive, and has a range of impressive features. This chapter looks at how to use the Edge browser to open web pages, use tabs, bookmarks and reading lists and add notes and annotations to pages.

Introducing the Edge Browser

The web browser Internet Explorer (IE) has been synonymous with Microsoft for almost as long as the Windows operating system. Introduced in 1995, shortly after Windows 95, it has been the default browser for a generation of web users. However, as with most technologies, the relentless march of time has caught up with IE, and although it is still included with Windows 10, the preferred browser is designed specifically for the digital mobile age. It is called Microsoft Edge, and adapts easily to whichever environment it is operating in: desktop, tablet or phone.

The Microsoft Edge browser has a number of performance and speed enhancements compared with IE, and it also recognizes that modern web users want a lot more from their browser than simply being able to look at web pages. It includes a function for drawing on and annotating web pages, which can then be sent to other people as screenshots.

There is also a Hub where you can store all of your favorites, downloads and pages that you have selected to read at a later date (which can be when you are offline if required).

Click on this icon from the **Taskbar** or the **Start** menu to open the Microsoft Edge browser at the default Start page.

Back/forward buttons   Refresh   Hub button   Toolbar buttons

More options

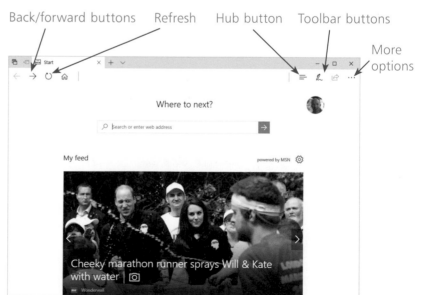

Beware

For details about connecting to a network, and the Internet, see pages 210-211.

Don't forget

Internet Explorer can still be used with Windows 10, and it will probably continue to be supported for a period of time.

Don't forget

The Start page also displays news information.

Hot tip

The Start page can be replaced by your own specific Homepage, see page 186 for details.

Smart Address Bar

Smart address bars are now a familiar feature in a lot of modern browsers, and Microsoft Edge is no different. This can be used to enter a specific web address, to open that page, or use it to search for a word or phrase. To use the smart address bar:

1 Click anywhere in the Start page address box or in the address box at the top of a web page

2 Start typing a word or website address. As you type, options appear below the address bar. Click on a web page address to open that website

3 Click on one of the options with a magnifying glass next to it to view the search result for that item

Hot tip

The personal digital assistant, Cortana, can also be used to open web pages, by asking it to open a specific page. The page will be opened in Microsoft Edge.

Hot tip

Search results are found through Microsoft's search engine, Bing. To change the default search engine click on **... (More Options) > Settings**. Then, select the **View advanced settings** button, click on the **Change search engine** button and select a new default search engine.

Hot tip

In the Windows 10 Creators Update, the Microsoft Edge browser has a Homepage button on the top toolbar. (If you can't see this, go to the Settings button in Step 3, then **View advanced settings**, and click the **Show the home button** option to On.)

Hot tip

Within the settings for Microsoft Edge there is an option for importing favorites from another web browser. To do this, click on the **Import from another browser** button in Step 3, select the required browser and click on the **Import** button.

Don't forget

If a specific Homepage is assigned, the Start page as shown on page 184 will not be displayed.

Setting a Homepage

By default, Microsoft Edge opens at its own Start page. This may not be ideal for most users, who will want to set their own Homepage that appears when Microsoft Edge is launched.

1 Click on this button on the top toolbar to access the menu options

2 Click on the **Settings** button

Settings

3 By default, the Start page is selected as the opening page

Settings	📌

Choose a theme

Light	⌄

Open Microsoft Edge with

Start page	⌄

Open new tabs with

Top sites and suggested content	⌄

Import favorites and other info

Import from another browser

4 Click here and select **A specific page or pages**

Start page

New tab page

Previous pages

A specific page or pages

5 Enter the website address you want to use as your Homepage, and click on the **Save** button

ineasysteps.com	✕	💾

Using Tabs

Being able to open several web pages at the same time in different tabs is now a common feature of web browsers. To do this with Microsoft Edge:

 Click on this button at the top of the Microsoft Edge window

 Pages can be opened in new tabs using the smart address bar or the list of **Top sites** that appears below it

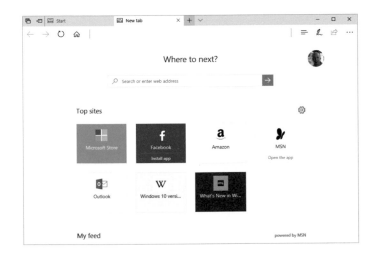

The Start page for new tabs, as displayed in Step 2, can be changed if required. To do this, open the Microsoft Edge Settings as shown on the previous page and change the selection under the **Open new tabs with** heading.

187

3 All open tabs are displayed at the top of the window. Click and hold on a tab to drag it into a new position

| 🗗 🗗 | 🖼 Start | | f Facebook - Log In or Sign U | In Easy Steps Smart Lea × | + |
| ← → ↺ ⌂ | ineasysteps.com |

| 🗗 🗗 | 🖼 Start | | In Easy Steps Smart Lea × | f Facebook - Log In or Sign U | + |
| ← → ↺ ⌂ | ineasysteps.com |

...cont'd

Tab previews

If there are a large number of tabs open it can be hard to remember exactly what is in each one. This is addressed in the Edge browser through the tab previews function. To use this:

Tabs previews is a new feature in the Windows 10 Creators Update.

 All open tabs are shown at the top of the browser, with the current active tab colored light gray

 Move the mouse cursor over one of the inactive tabs to view a preview of the content within it

 Click on this button next to the New Tab button to view thumbnails of all of the current tabs

 Thumbnails of all of the current tabs are displayed. Click on one to view it, or click on this button to close the preview panel

...cont'd

Set aside tabs

To avoid the Edge browser window becoming too cluttered with open tabs at the top of it, it is possible to set aside the current tabs so that they are stored together, but not along the top of the browser window. To do this:

1 All open tabs are shown at the top of the browser

Set aside tabs is a new feature in the Windows 10 Creators Update.

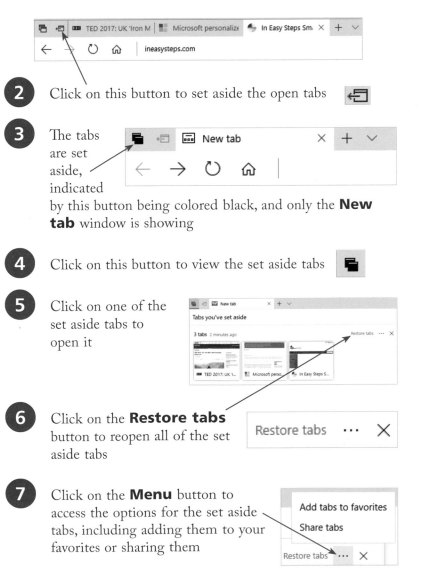

2 Click on this button to set aside the open tabs

3 The tabs are set aside, indicated by this button being colored black, and only the **New tab** window is showing

4 Click on this button to view the set aside tabs

5 Click on one of the set aside tabs to open it

6 Click on the **Restore tabs** button to reopen all of the set aside tabs

Restore tabs   ···   ✕

7 Click on the **Menu** button to access the options for the set aside tabs, including adding them to your favorites or sharing them

Add tabs to favorites

Share tabs

Restore tabs ··· ✕

Bookmarking Web Pages

Your favorite web pages can be bookmarked so that you can access them with one click from the Hub area, rather than having to enter the web address each time. To do this:

1 Open the web page that you want to bookmark

2 Click on this button on the toolbar

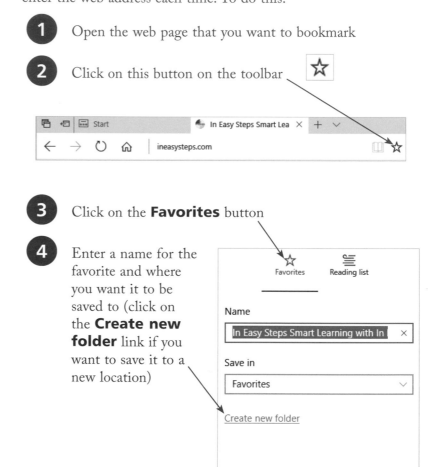

Hot tip

The Favorites bar can be displayed underneath the Address bar by opening the Microsoft Edge **Settings** and dragging the **Show the favorites bar** button to **On**.

3 Click on the **Favorites** button

4 Enter a name for the favorite and where you want it to be saved to (click on the **Create new folder** link if you want to save it to a new location)

5 Click on the **Add** button

6 The star button turns yellow, indicating that the web page has been added as a Favorite

7 Click on this button to access your Favorites (see page 193)

Adding Notes to Web Pages

One of the innovations in the Microsoft Edge browser is the ability to draw on and annotate web pages. This can be useful to highlight parts of a web page or add your own comments and views, which can then be sent to other people. To add notes:

1 Open a web page to which you want to add a note or draw on, and click on this button on the toolbar of the Microsoft Edge browser

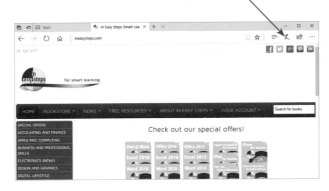

2 Click on one of the pen options

3 Make selections for the pen style, including color and size

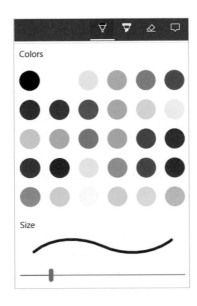

 Don't forget

Click on this button on the Notes toolbar to create a web clipping. This is an area of a web page that is selected by dragging over it to make the selection.

191

 Don't forget

Click on this button on the Notes toolbar to Save a web note or clipping. These can then be accessed from the Favorites section of Microsoft Edge (see page 193).

...cont'd

 Click and drag on the web page to draw over it

 Click on the eraser icon and drag over any items that you have drawn to remove them, or part of them

 Click on the text icon to add your own text

 Drag over the web page to create a text box

 Type the text that you want displayed on the web page

Look at some of these!

 Click and drag here on a text box to move its position in the window

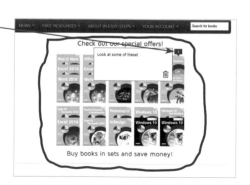

Organizing with the Hub

The Hub is the area where you can store a variety of items for the Microsoft Edge browser; from your favorite web pages to pages that you want to read offline at a later date. To use the Hub:

1 Click on this button to open the Hub

2 Click on this button to view your Favorites. Click on one to go to that page

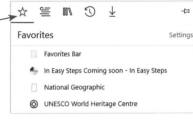

Hot tip

The Favorites window also has an option for importing favorites from other web browsers. Click on the **Settings** button and click on **Import from another browser** link, select the required browser and click on the **Import** button.

3 Click on this button to view your Reading list of pages that you have saved to read offline, or at a later date (see next page for details)

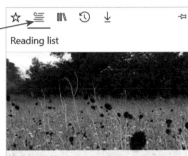

Why wildflower meadows are so special
bbc.com

Hot tip

Click on the **Books** button within the Hub to view any books that have been downloaded from the Windows Store and read them in the Edge browser.

4 Click on this button to view your web browsing history

5 Click on **Clear all history** to remove the items in the history

6 Click on this button to view items that you have downloaded from the web, such as PDF documents or apps (although not those from the Windows Store)

Browsing data can also be cleared from within Edge **Settings**. Under **Clear browsing data**, click on the **Choose what to clear** button, check **On** the items you want to clear and click on the **Clear** button.

Reading List

With some web pages you may want to save the content so that you can read it at a later date. If you make the page a favorite, the content could change the next time you look at it. Instead, you can add the page to your Reading list to ensure that you can read the same content. Also, you have the advantage of being able to access the items in your Reading list when you are offline and not connected to the internet. To do this:

 Open the web page that you want to add to the Reading list

 Click on this button on the Edge toolbar

 Click on the **Reading list** button

Hot tip

The Reading list is an excellent option if you are traveling and do not have internet access. You can save numerous articles in the Reading list and access them even when you are offline.

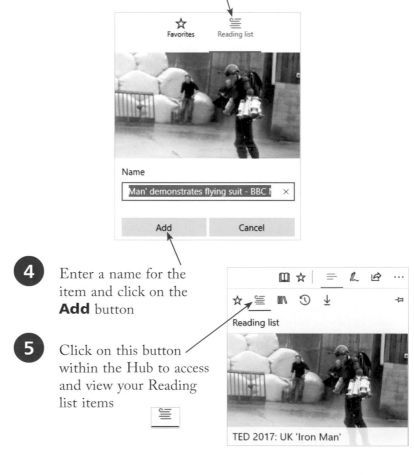

4 Enter a name for the item and click on the **Add** button

5 Click on this button within the Hub to access and view your Reading list items

Reading View

Modern web pages contain a lot more items than just text and pictures: video clips, pop-up ads, banners, and more contribute to the multimedia effect on many web pages. At times this additional content can enhance the page, but a lot of the time it is a distraction. If you want to just concentrate on the main item on a web page you can do this with the Reading view function:

1 Open the web page that you want to view in Reading view

2 Click on this button on the Microsoft Edge toolbar

3 The text and pictures are presented on a new page, with any additional content removed. Click on the buttons at the bottom to move through the content

New Zealand earthquake gives unexpected benefit

www.bbc.co.uk
1 min read

4 Click on this button again to return to the standard page view

Beware

Not all web pages support the Reading view functionality. If it is not supported, the button in Step 2 will be grayed-out.

More Options

There is no traditional menu bar in Microsoft Edge, but more options can be accessed from the right-hand toolbar:

 Click on this button to access the options

2 Click here to open a new browsing window, or a **New InPrivate window** which does not record any of your browsing history

AdBlock

New window

New InPrivate window

Zoom — 95% +

Cast media to device

Find on page

Print

Pin this page to Start

F12 Developer Tools

Open with Internet Explorer

Send feedback

Extensions

What's new and tips

Settings

3 Click on the **Zoom** button to increase or decrease the magnification of the page being viewed

4 Click on the **Find on page** button to search for a specific word or phrase on the web page

 Click on the **Print** button to print the current web page

 Click on the **Open with Internet Explorer** button to open the current web page in Microsoft Edge's predecessor

10 Keeping in Touch

This chapter looks at communicating via the Mail, People, Skype and Calendar apps.

Setting Up Mail

Email has become an essential part of everyday life, both socially and in the business world. Windows 10 accommodates this with the Mail app. This can be used to link to online services such as Gmail and Outlook (the renamed version of Hotmail) and also other email accounts. To set up an email account with Mail:

1 Click on the **Mail** app on the Start menu

2 Click on the **Accounts** button

3 Click on the **Add account** button

Hot tip

The **Other account** option in Step 4 can be used to add a non-webmail account. This is usually a POP3 account and you will need your email address, username, password, and usually the incoming and outgoing email servers. If you do not know these, they should be supplied by your email provider. They should also be available in the Account settings of the email account you want to add to the Mail app.

4 Select the type of account to which you want to link via the Mail app. This can be an online email account that you have already set up

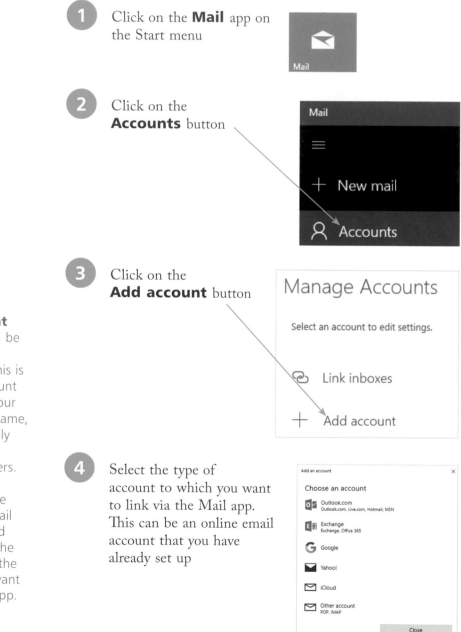

5 Enter your current sign in details for the selected email account and click on the **Sign in** button

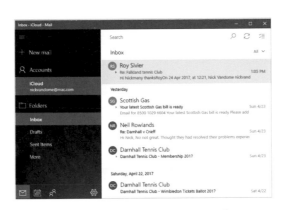

You can add more than one account to the Mail app. If you do this, you will be able to select the different accounts to view within Mail.

6 Once it has been connected, the details of the account are shown under the Mail heading, including the mailboxes within the account. Click on the **Inbox** to view the emails within it

7 The list of emails appears in the main window. Double-click on an email to view it at full size

Working with Mail

Once you have set up an account in the Mail app you can then start creating and managing your emails with it.

 On the Inbox page, open an email and click on the **Reply**, **Reply all** or **Forward** buttons to respond

← Reply   ≪ Reply all   → Forward

 Open an email and click on the **Delete** button to remove it

🗑 Delete

Composing email

To compose and send an email message:

 Click on this button to create a new message

+ New mail

 Click in the **To** field and enter an email address

Sent from Mail for Windows 10

 Click on the **Cc & Bcc** link to access options for blind copying

Don't forget

Contacts that are added automatically as email recipients are taken from the People app, providing there is an email address connected to their entry.

4 The email address can either be in the format of myname@email.com, or enter the name of one of your contacts from the People app and the email address will be entered automatically

...cont'd

5 Enter a subject heading and body text to the email

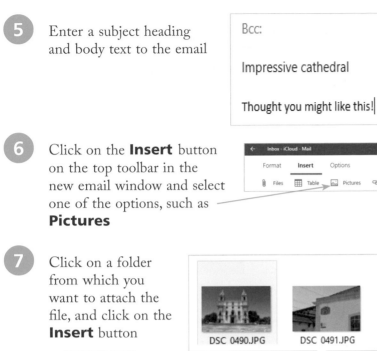

Bcc:

Impressive cathedral

Thought you might like this!

6 Click on the **Insert** button on the top toolbar in the new email window and select one of the options, such as **Pictures**

7 Click on a folder from which you want to attach the file, and click on the **Insert** button

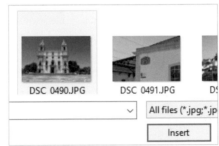

DSC 0490.JPG   DSC 0491.JPG   DS

Insert

All files (*.jpg;*.jp

Insert

8 The file is shown in the body of the email

Impressive cathedral

Thought you might like this!

Sent from Mail for Windows 10

9 Select an item of text and select the text formatting options from the top toolbar

| Format | Insert | Options | | | | 🗑 Discard | ▷ Send |

B *I* U A ⌄ ≔ ≕ ≡ ⌄ Heading 1 ⌄ ↶ Undo ↷ Redo

10 Click on this button to send the email

▷ Send

Chatting with Skype

Skype is one of the premier services for free video and voice calls (to other Skype users) and instant messaging for text messages. It can now be incorporated into your Windows 10 experience and used to keep in touch with family, friends and work colleagues at home and around the world.

If the Skype button is not available on the Start menu, the app can be downloaded from the Windows Store.

Hot tip

If you are signed in to your PC with your Microsoft Account details then you will be able to use Skype without having to first sign in.

1 Click on the **Skype** button on the Start menu

2 If you already have a Skype account you can sign in with these details, or with your Microsoft account details. Click on **Create a new account** to create a new Skype account

Welcome to the Skype

Sign in using your Skype or Microsoft account to experience the next generation of Skype for Windows 10. It's simpler, faster and packed with great new features.

Skype or Microsoft account

Create a new account

3 Once you have entered your Skype login details you can check your speakers, microphone and webcam for voice and video calls. Click on the **Sign In** button

Sign In

4 Recent conversation are listed in the left-hand panel, or contacts can be selected to start a new conversation (see next page)

5 Click on this button to view your Skype contacts. Tap on one to start a voice or video call or text message

6 Click in the **Search Skype directory** box to look for other Skype contacts

7 Select a contact and click in this box to start a text conversation

8 Select a contact and click on the phone button to make a voice call or the video button to make a video call

When you create a text conversation with one of your contacts in Skype, it will continue down the page as you respond to each other.

When you add someone as a contact you have to send them a contact request, which they must accept to become one of your contacts.

Do not accept requests from people you don't know. If you receive one of these, click on **Decline** when they send you a request.

203

Finding People

An electronic address book is always a good feature to have on a computer, and with Windows 10 this function is provided by the People app. This not only allows you to add your own contacts manually, you can also link to any of your online accounts, such as Gmail or iCloud, and import the contacts that you have there. To do this:

 Click on the **People** app on the Start menu

 The current contacts are displayed. By default, these will be linked to your Microsoft Account, if you have created one

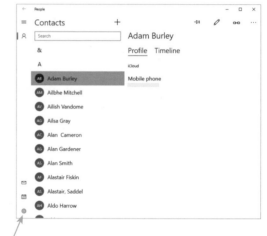

Click on the **Settings** button to add new accounts from which you want to import contacts, such as a Gmail or an iCloud account (in the same way as setting up a new email account). Click on the **Add an account** button to add the required account: the contacts from the linked account are imported to the People app

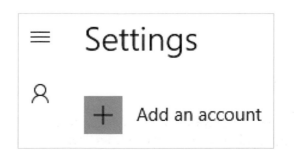

Adding contacts manually

As well as importing contacts, it is also possible to enter them manually into the People app:

1 Click on this button at the top of the **People** app

2 Enter details for the new contact, including name, email address and phone number

> **Hot tip**
>
> To delete a contact, right-click on their name in the Contacts list and click on the **Delete** button to remove it.

3 Click on the Down arrow next to a field to access additional options for that item

> **Hot tip**
>
> Once a contact has been added, select it as in Step 2 on the previous page and click on this button to edit the contact's details.
>
>

4 Click on the **Save** button at the top of the window to create the new contact

Save

Using the Calendar

The Calendar app can be used to record important events and reminders. To view the calendar:

 1 Click on the **Calendar** app on the Start menu, or access it from **All apps**

Calendar

2 Click on the **Settings** button

3 Click on the **Manage Accounts** button to add or delete a calendar account

Settings

Manage Accounts

Accounts can be added to the Calendar app in the same way as for the Mail and People apps.

206

4 Click here to view specific months and click on the top toolbar to view by **Year**

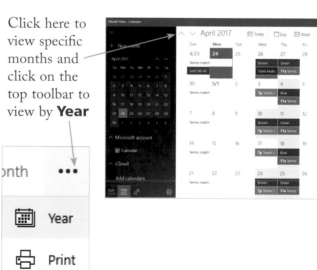

onth · · ·

▦ Year

🖶 Print

5 Click on these buttons to move between months (or swipe left or right on a touchpad)

...cont'd

Adding events

Events can be added to the calendar and various settings can be
applied to them, such as recurrence and reminders.

 Click on a date to create a new event
or click on the **New event** button

+ New event

Reminders can be set
for calendar events,
and these appear in the
Notifications section.
Click on this box on the
top toolbar to set a time
period for a reminder.

Reminder: | 12 hours ✓

2 Enter an **Event name** and a **Location**
at the top of the window

3 Click on the **Start** field and enter a date and time for
the event

| Start: June 14, 2017 | 📅 | 4:00 PM ✓ | ☐ All day |
| End: June 14, 2017 | 📅 | 6:00 PM ✓ | |

4 If **All day** is selected, the time in the **Start** and **End**
fields will be grayed-out

| Start: June 14, 2017 | 📅 | 12:00 AM ✓ | ☑ All day |
| End: June 14, 2017 | 📅 | 12:00 AM ✓ | |

207

...cont'd

5 For a recurring event, click on the **Repeat** button on the top toolbar

 Select an option for the recurrence, such as **Weekly** and select a day for the recurrence

Repeat

Start: June 14, 2017 ✕ 📅

Weekly ⌄

Every 1 ⌄ week(s) on

☐ Sun ☐ Mon ☐ Tue ✔ Wed

☐ Thu ☐ Fri ☐ Sat

End: Never 📅

When an event is due, an alert will appear on the screen.

7 Click on the **Save and close** button in the main window to save the event

🖼 Save and close

8 To delete an existing event, move the cursor over it and click on the **Edit occurrence** button

Tennis match

🧑 4/23/2017 - 4/24/2017, All day
Home

Edit series   Edit occurrence

9 Click on the **Delete** button

🗑 Delete

11 Networking

Windows 10 has a built-in networking capability, so that a variety of items can be shared between two or more computers. This chapter shows how to set this up.

Network Components

There are numerous possibilities for setting up a home network. To start with, there are two major network technologies:

- **Wired** – e.g. Ethernet, using twisted pair cables to send data at rates of 10, 100 or 1000 Mbps (megabits per second).

- **Wireless** – using radio waves to send data at rates of 11 to 300 Mbps, or up to, in theory, 1 Gbps with the latest devices (although all of these are theoretical top speeds).

There is also a variety of hardware items required:

- **Network adapter** – appropriate to the network type, with one for each computer in the network.

- **Network controller** – one or more hub, switch or router, providing the actual connection to each network adapter.

There is also the internet connection (dial-up, DSL or cable), using:

- A modem connected to one of the computers.

- A modem connected to the network.

- Internet access incorporated into the router or switch.

Setting up the components

The steps you will need, and the most appropriate sequence to follow, will depend on the specific options on your system. However, the main steps will include:

- Install network adapters in the computers, where necessary (in most cases these will be pre-installed in the computer).

- Set up or verify the internet connection (this should be provided by your Internet Service Provider (ISP).

- Configure the wireless router or access point (this could involve installing software for the router, which may be provided on a CD or DVD. Some routers will be automatically recognized by the Windows 10 Creators Update).

- Start up Windows on your PC.

The Windows 10 Creators Update is designed to automate as much of the network setup task as possible.

The network adapter can be connected to the USB port, inserted in the PC Card slot or installed inside your computer.

Ethernet adapters connect to a network hub, switch or wired router. Wireless adapters connect through a wireless router or a combination of router/switch.

210

You may already have some of these elements in operation, if you have an existing network running a previous version of Windows.

Connecting to a Network

You can connect your computers to form a network using Ethernet cables and adapters, or by setting up your wireless adapters and routers. When you start up each computer, Windows 10 will examine the current configuration and discover any new networks that have been established since the last start up. You can check this, or connect manually to a network, from within the Wi-Fi settings from the Network & Internet section of Settings. To do this:

1 Access the **Settings** app and click on the **Network & Internet** button

2 Drag the Wi-Fi button to **On**. Under the **Wi-Fi** heading, click on one of the available networks

3 Click on the network and drag **On** the **Connect automatically when in range** button

4 The selected network is shown as **Connected**. This is also shown in the Notification area

Beware

The most common type of network for connecting to is the internet.

Beware

If your network is unavailable for any reason, this will be noted in Step 2.

Viewing Network Status

Once you have connected to a network, and usually the internet too, you can view your current network status. To do this:

 Access the **Settings** app and select **Network & Internet**. Click on the **Status** button in the left-hand panel

 The currently connected network is shown under **Network status** (this will normally be your Wi-Fi connection to the internet)

Status

Network status

PlusnetWireless792287

You're connected to the Internet
If you have a limited data plan, you can make this network a metered connection or change other properties.

 Click on **Change connection properties** to view the settings for the current network connection

Change connection properties

4 The properties for the current network connection are displayed. Drag the **Make this PC discoverable** button to **On** to enable other devices to see your PC on a network

⚙ PlusnetWireless792287

Connect automatically when in range

On

Make this PC discoverable

Allow your PC to be discoverable by other PCs and devices on this network. We recommend turning this on for private networks at home or work, but turning it off for public networks to help keep your stuff safe.

On

Metered connection

If you have a limited data plan and want more control over data usage, make this connection a metered connection. Some apps might work differently to reduce data usage when you're connected to this network.

Set as metered connection

Off

5 To reduce data usage, drag the **Set as metered connection** button from **Off** to **On**. This can be used if you have a limited data Wi-Fi service, and Windows will make system changes to reduce overall network traffic

...cont'd

6 On the main Status page, click on **Change adapter options** for your network adapter

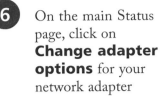

Change your network settings

Change adapter options
View network adapters and change connection settings.

7 Details of the network connections are displayed

If a network connection in Step 7 has a red cross on it, this indicates that the connection is not active. However, its details can still be viewed, as with an active connection.

8 Click on one of the network connections to view its details, including Signal Quality

Wi-Fi Status

General

Connection
IPv4 Connectivity: Internet
IPv6 Connectivity: No network access
Media State: Enabled
SSID: PlusnetWireless792287
Duration: 12 days 01:51:19
Speed: 130.0 Mbps
Signal Quality:

Details... Wireless Properties

Activity
Sent — Received
Bytes: 41,017,849 | 666,289,800

Properties Disable Diagnose

Close

213

9 On the main Status page, click on **View your network properties**

View your network properties

10 Details of the network properties are displayed

View your network properties

Properties
Name: Ethernet
Description: Broadcom NetLink (TM) Gigabit Ethernet
Physical address (MAC): 20:89:84:6a:fb:58
Status: Not operational
Maximum transmission unit: 1500
IPv4 address: 169.254.208.34/16
IPv6 address: fe80::2d9a:ed59:8b13:d022%17/64
DNS servers: 150.200.3.2
Connectivity (IPv4/IPv6): Disconnected

Name: Local Area Connection* 1
Description: Microsoft Wi-Fi Direct Virtual Adapter

Some of the details in Step 10 can be useful for certain technical details if you need to contact your Internet Service Provider. One of these is the MAC address of the computer.

Join the HomeGroup

The HomeGroup is a network function that enables a Windows 10 computer to connect to another Windows 10 machine (or Windows 7/8) and share content. You can set up and connect to the HomeGroup through the Settings app:

Don't forget

When you add a computer to your network, Windows 10 on that computer will detect that there is a HomeGroup already created.

Beware

A HomeGroup applies to any user with an account on the computer, so if a different user logs on, the associated files will also be accessible.

Don't forget

Windows generates the password when the HomeGroup is created. If you forget the password, you can find it in the Control Panel on any computer already joined to the HomeGroup.

1 Access **Network & Internet > Status** in the Settings app and click on the **HomeGroup** link (which opens in the Control Panel)

2 Click on the **Create a homegroup** button to start setting up the HomeGroup

3 Click the **Next** button

4 Select the items that you want to share in the HomeGroup and click on the **Next** button

5 Enter the password from the other computer. Click on the **Finish** button. Once you have joined the HomeGroup you will be able to share your files on the other computer, and vice versa

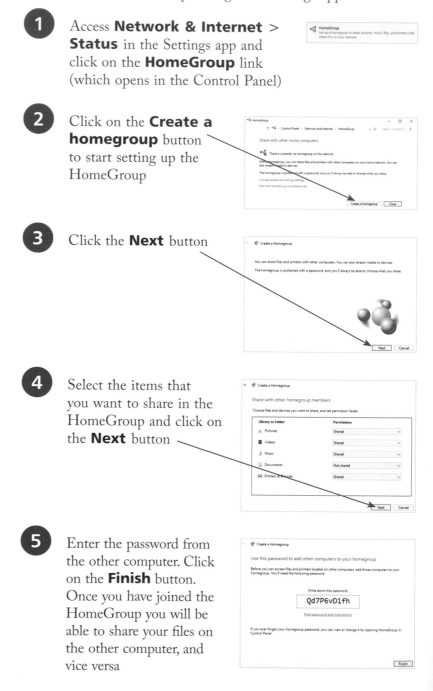

Sharing Files and Folders

There are different ways in which you can share items once a HomeGroup has been set up:

 1 Open File Explorer and select the **HomeGroup** in the Navigation pane, then click on the **Share libraries and devices** button in the HomeGroup section of the File Explorer Ribbon tabs

2 Select the items that you want to share with the HomeGroup. This will be done automatically, i.e. if you share Pictures then all of the items in the Pictures library will be shared, as will new ones that are added in the future

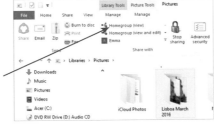

The **Share with** section in File Explorer is accessed from the Share tab on the Ribbon.

215

3 To share a specific item, select it in File Explorer and click on the **HomeGroup (view)** button in the Share with section

4 Select HomeGroup in the Navigation pane of the File Explorer pane to view the shared item in Step 3

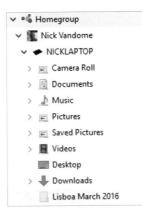

Sharing Settings

Within the Network and Sharing Center there are also options for specifying how items are shared over the network, not just in the HomeGroup. To select these:

1 Open **Settings** > **Network & Internet** > **Status** and click on the **Sharing options** link

Sharing options
For the networks you connect to, decide what you want to share.

2 Select sharing options for different networks, including Private, Guest or Public, and All networks. Options can be selected for turning on network discovery so that your computer can see other computers on the network, and file and printer sharing

If you are sharing over a network you should be able to access the Public folder on another computer (providing that network discovery is turned on). If you are the administrator of the other computer you will also be able to access your own Home folder, although you will need to enter the required password for this.

Advanced sharing settings

↑ « Network and Sharing Center › Advanced sharing settings ⌄ ↻ Search Control P... 🔎

Change sharing options for different network profiles
Windows creates a separate network profile for each network you use. You can choose specific options for each profile.

Private (current profile)

Network discovery

When network discovery is on, this computer can see other network computers and devices and is visible to other network computers.

● Turn on network discovery
☑ Turn on automatic setup of network connected devices.
○ Turn off network discovery

File and printer sharing

When file and printer sharing is on, files and printers that you have shared from this computer can be accessed by people on the network.

● Turn on file and printer sharing
○ Turn off file and printer sharing

Save changes   Cancel

3 Click on these arrows to expand the options for each network category

Change sharing options for different network profiles
Windows creates a separate network profile for each network you use. You can choose specific options for each profile.

Private (current profile)   ⌄

Guest or Public   ⌄

All Networks   ⌃

Public folder sharing

When Public folder sharing is on, people on the network, including homegroup members, can access files in the Public folders.

○ Turn on sharing so anyone with network access can read and write files in the Public folders
● Turn off Public folder sharing (people logged on to this computer can still access these folders)

View Network Components

You can also view the components of the network in File Explorer. To do this:

 1 Open File Explorer and click on the **Network** library

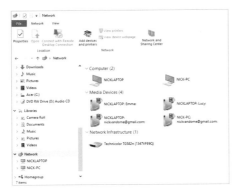

 2 To view the shared items offered by a particular computer, for example Nick-PC, double-click on the associated icon

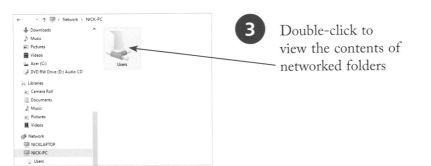

3 Double-click to view the contents of networked folders

Don't forget

The Public folder on your own computer can be used to make items available to other users on the network.

Public files and folders, plus those belonging to the currently-active user, are available to access. Items can be copied here for sharing purposes.

Network Troubleshooting

 Open **Settings** > **Network & Internet** > **Status** and click on the **Network troubleshooter** link

⚠ Network troubleshooter
Diagnose and fix network problems.

For more Windows 10 troubleshooting options, see page 221.

 Click on the option that most closely matches your network problem

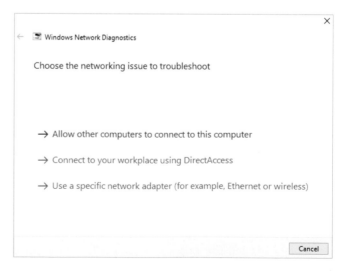

×

← 🖥 Windows Network Diagnostics

What type of networking problems are you having?

Windows tested your Internet connection and verified that you are able to access some websites. Are you looking for help with a different issue?

→ I'm trying to reach a specific website or folder on a network

→ I'm having a different problem
   Show me other network troubleshooting options.

Cancel

 Most options have additional selections that can be made to try to solve the problem. Click on these as required

×

← 🖥 Windows Network Diagnostics

Choose the networking issue to troubleshoot

→ Allow other computers to connect to this computer

→ Connect to your workplace using DirectAccess

→ Use a specific network adapter (for example, Ethernet or wireless)

Cancel

12 System and Security

Windows 10 includes tools to help protect your online privacy, troubleshoot common problems, maintain your hard drive, protect your computer from malicious software, back up your files, folders and apps, and keep your system up-to-date.

The **Privacy** options have been enhanced in the Windows 10 Creators Update, and there is a range of privacy settings that can be applied when the Creators Update is first installed.

Click on **Privacy Statement** in Step 2 to view Microsoft's Privacy Statement (this is an online statement and, by default, displayed within the Edge browser).

The Privacy Settings also have a range of options for enabling, or disabling, location access to specific apps.

Privacy

Online privacy is a major issue for all computer users, and the Windows 10 Creators Update has a number of options for viewing details about your personal online privacy.

1 Open the **Settings** app and click on the **Privacy** button

🔒

Privacy
Location, camera

2 Drag these buttons **On** or **Off** to allow advertising more specific to you, let websites provide local content based on the language being used by Windows and let Windows track apps that are launched to make the search results more specific

General

Change privacy options

Let apps use advertising ID to make ads more interesting to you based on your app usage (turning this off will reset your ID)
⬤ On

Let websites provide locally relevant content by accessing my language list
⬤ On

Let Windows track app launches to improve Start and search results
⬤ On

Manage my info that's stored in the cloud

Privacy Statement

3 Click on **Manage my info that's stored in the cloud** to view details on the Microsoft website about how ads are used online and in Windows 10 apps

To opt out of personalized ads in this browser, your browser history must allow first-party and third-party cookies and you must have your browsing experience set to NOT delete browsing history on exit. Instructions for enabling cookies and configuring your browsing history may be available in your browser's settings, privacy, or help documentation.   ✕

▪ Microsoft   Sign in

About Our Ads

To create a more customized online experience, some of the ads you may receive on Microsoft websites and apps are tailored to your previous activities, searches and site visits. You're in control and here's where you can make the advertising choice that's right for you.

Where Can I Learn More about Advertising on Microsoft Websites and Apps?

Microsoft partners with AOL, AppNexus and other third party service providers to help present customized content and display advertisements on MSN, Outlook.com and other websites and apps. Microsoft also delivers search ads to Bing and our search syndication partners. Learn more about Microsoft's privacy practices here. You can learn more about interest-based ads from AOL and AppNexus in their privacy statements: AOL and AppNexus.

Personalized ads in this browser
ON ⬤
Control the "personalized ads" setting for this web browser.

Learn more

4 Drag the **Personalized ads in this browser** button to **On** to control the types of ads that are displayed in your browser

Personalized ads in this browser
ON ⬤

Control the "personalized ads" setting for this web browser.

Learn more ⌄

5 Click on **Learn more** in Step 2 to view further details about general privacy settings and options within Windows 10

Know your privacy options

Learn how this setting impacts your privacy.
Learn more

Troubleshooting

On any computing system there are always things that go wrong or do not work properly. The Windows 10 Creators Update is no different, but there are comprehensive troubleshooting options for trying to address a range of problems. To use this:

1 Open the **Settings** app, select **Update & security** and click on the **Troubleshoot** button

2 The range of troubleshooting options is displayed within the main window

The **Troubleshooting** options have been enhanced in the Windows 10 Creators Update.

3 The top troubleshooting categories are displayed at the top of the window (other options are shown further down the window)

Get up and running

Internet Connections
Find and fix problems with connecting to the Internet or to websites.

Playing Audio
Find and fix problems with playing sound.

Printer
Find and fix problems with printing.

Windows Update
Resolve problems that prevent you from updating Windows.

4 Click on one of the categories to select it, and click on the **Run the troubleshooter** button

Playing Audio
Find and fix problems with playing sound.

Run the troubleshooter

5 Any issues for the selected item are displayed, and options for trying to fix the issue

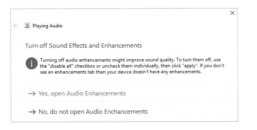

System Properties

There are several ways to open the System Properties, and view information about your computer:

1 Select **Settings** > **System** > **About**
or

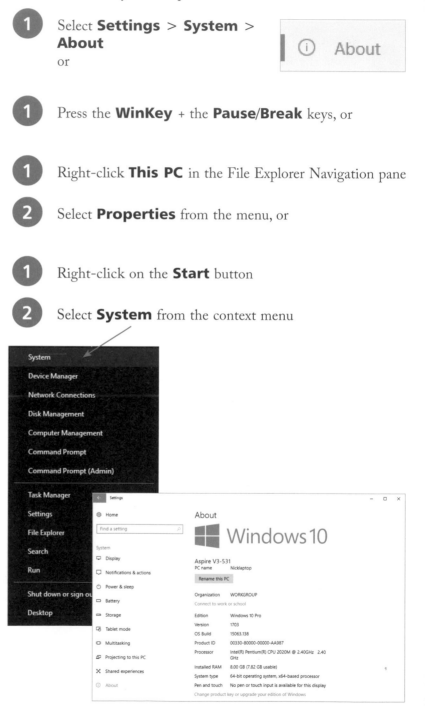

ⓘ About

1 Press the **WinKey** + the **Pause/Break** keys, or

1 Right-click **This PC** in the File Explorer Navigation pane

2 Select **Properties** from the menu, or

1 Right-click on the **Start** button

2 Select **System** from the context menu

Don't forget

The main System panel provides the Windows 10 edition, processor details, memory size, computer and network names, and Windows 10 activation status. There are also links to the Device Manager and to more advanced settings.

System
Device Manager
Network Connections
Disk Management
Computer Management
Command Prompt
Command Prompt (Admin)

Task Manager
Settings
File Explorer
Search
Run

Shut down or sign out
Desktop

Settings

⌂ Home

Find a setting

System
- ☐ Display
- ☐ Notifications & actions
- ⏻ Power & sleep
- ☐ Battery
- ☐ Storage
- ☐ Tablet mode
- ☐ Multitasking
- ☐ Projecting to this PC
- ✕ Shared experiences
- ⓘ About

About

Windows 10

Aspire V3-531
PC name   Nicklaptop
Rename this PC

Organization   WORKGROUP
Connect to work or school

Edition   Windows 10 Pro
Version   1703
OS Build   15063.138
Product ID   00330-80000-00000-AA987
Processor   Intel(R) Pentium(R) CPU 2020M @ 2.40GHz   2.40 GHz
Installed RAM   8.00 GB (7.82 GB usable)
System type   64-bit operating system, x64-based processor
Pen and touch   No pen or touch input is available for this display

Change product key or upgrade your edition of Windows

Device Manager

1 Select **Settings** > **System** > **About** > **Device Manager** to list all of the hardware components that are installed on your computer

Related settings
Additional administrative tools
BitLocker settings
Device Manager

2 Select the › symbol to expand that entry to show details

3 Double-click any device to open its properties

Device Manager
File   Action   View   Help
⬅ ➡ | 🖮 | 🔢 🖮 | 🖳
∨ 🖥 Nicklaptop
  > 🎙 Audio inputs and outputs
  > 🔋 Batteries
  > ⓑ Bluetooth
  > 💻 Computer
  > — Disk drives
  > 🖵 Display adapters
  > 💿 DVD/CD-ROM drives
  > 🕮 Human Interface Devices
  > 🖭 IDE ATA/ATAPI controllers
  > 🔅 Imaging devices
  > ⌨ Keyboards
  > 🖱 Mice and other pointing devices
  > 🖵 Monitors
  > 🖧 Network adapters
  > 🖅 Other devices
  > 🖶 Print queues
  > ▯ Processors
  > 💾 SD host adapters
  > ▮ Software devices
  > 🔊 Sound, video and game controllers
  > 🖴 Storage controllers
  > 🖿 System devices
  > 🖊 Universal Serial Bus controllers

Intel(R) HD Graphics Properties   ✕

General   Driver   Details   Events   Resources

🖵 Intel(R) HD Graphics

Device type: Display adapters
Manufacturer: Intel Corporation
Location: PCI bus 0, device 2, function 0

Device status
This device is working properly.

                                    OK   Cancel

4 Select the ⌄ symbol to collapse the expanded entry

You may be prompted for an administrator password or asked for permission to continue, when you select some Device Manager entries.

5 Select the Driver tab and select **Update Driver** to find and install new software

6 Select **Disable Device** to put the particular device offline. The button changes to **Enable Device**, to reverse the action

Enable Device

Intel(R) HD Graphics Properties   ✕

General   Driver   Details   Events   Resources

🖵 Intel(R) HD Graphics

Driver Provider: Intel Corporation
Driver Date: 12/21/2015
Driver Version: 10.18.10.4358
Digital Signer: Microsoft Windows Hardware Compatibility
                   Publisher

Driver Details   View details about the installed driver files.

Update Driver   Update the driver for this device.

Roll Back Driver   If the device fails after updating the driver, roll
                   back to the previously installed driver.

Disable Device   Disable the device.

Uninstall Device   Uninstall the device from the system (Advanced).

                                    OK   Cancel

Click on the **Roll Back Driver** button to switch back to the previously-installed driver for that device, if the new one fails.

Clean Up Your Disk

 In File Explorer, right-click the **C:** drive and click on the **Properties** option

 Click on the **Disk Cleanup** button

3 Disk Cleanup scans the drive to identify files that can be safely removed

4 All of the possible files are listed by category, and the sets of files recommended to be deleted are marked with a tick symbol

5 Make changes to the selections, clicking **View Files** if necessary to help you choose

6 Select the **Clean up system files** button, to also include these, then select **OK**

 Deleted files will not be transferred to the Recycle Bin, so confirm that you do want to permanently delete all of these files. The files will be removed and the disk space will become available

Don't forget

You can have more than one hard disk on your computer.

When a file is written to the hard disk, it may be stored in several pieces in different places. This fragmentation of disk space can slow down your computer. Disk Defragmenter rearranges the data so the disk will work more efficiently.

1 In the File Explorer, right-click on the **C:** drive and click on the **Properties** option

2 Select the **Tools** tab and click on the **Optimize** button

3 The process runs as a scheduled task, but you can select a drive and select **Analyze** to check out a new drive

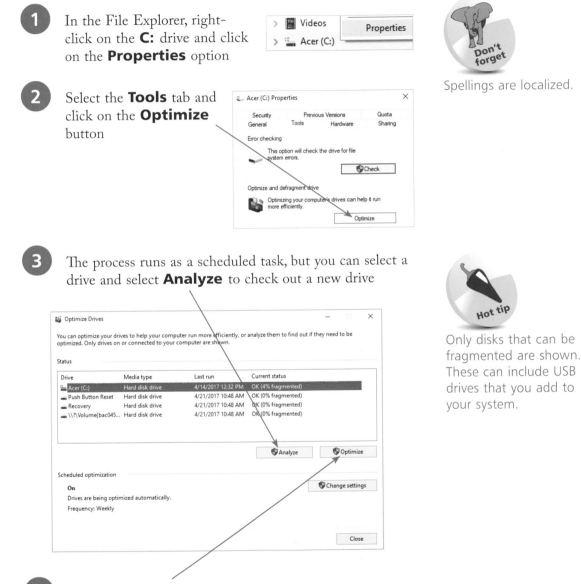

4 Click the **Optimize** button to process the selected disk drive. This may take between several minutes to several hours to complete, depending on the size and state of the disk, but you can still use your computer while the task is running

Spellings are localized.

Only disks that can be fragmented are shown. These can include USB drives that you add to your system.

Windows Update

Updates to Windows 10 and other Microsoft products are supplied regularly to help prevent or fix problems, improve the security or enhance performance. The way in which they are downloaded and installed can be specified from the Settings app:

1 Access the **Settings** app and click on the **Update & security** button

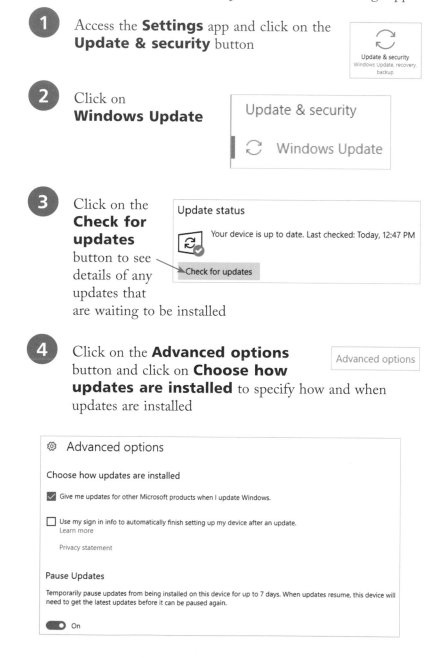

2 Click on **Windows Update**

Update & security

Windows Update

3 Click on the **Check for updates** button to see details of any updates that are waiting to be installed

Update status

Your device is up to date. Last checked: Today, 12:47 PM

Check for updates

4 Click on the **Advanced options** button and click on **Choose how updates are installed** to specify how and when updates are installed

Advanced options

⚙ Advanced options

Choose how updates are installed

☑ Give me updates for other Microsoft products when I update Windows.

☐ Use my sign in info to automatically finish setting up my device after an update.
Learn more

Privacy statement

Pause Updates

Temporarily pause updates from being installed on this device for up to 7 days. When updates resume, this device will need to get the latest updates before it can be paused again.

⬤ On

Hot tip

Click on the **Windows Insider Program** link within the **Update & security** settings to access pre-release versions of the latest Windows 10 updates.

NEW

Pausing updates is a new feature in the Windows 10 Creators Update.

Hot tip

To avoid being inundated with updates, under **Pause Updates** in Step 4, drag the button to **On** to prevent updates being installed for up to 7 days. However, updates should still be installed regularly to ensure that the latest security updates are installed.

Backing Up

Backing up your data is an important task in any computer environment, and in the Windows 10 Creators Update this can be done from within the Settings app. To do this:

1 Access the **Settings** app and click on the **Update & security** button

2 Click on the **Backup** button

⬆ Backup

3 Click on the **Add a drive** button to select an external drive for the backup

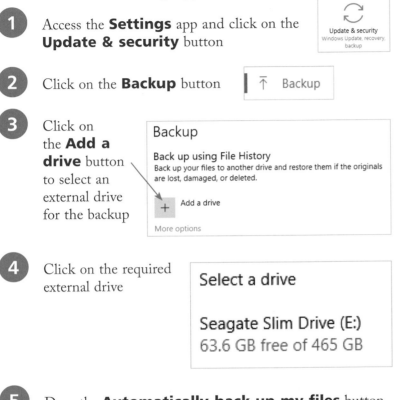

Backup

Back up using File History
Back up your files to another drive and restore them if the originals are lost, damaged, or deleted.

➕ Add a drive

More options

4 Click on the required external drive

Select a drive

Seagate Slim Drive (E:)
63.6 GB free of 465 GB

5 Drag the **Automatically back up my files** button to **On** to back up your files whenever the external drive is connected. After the initial backup, each further one will be incremental, i.e. only new files that have been added or changed will be backed up, not the whole system

Backup

Back up using File History
Back up your files to another drive and restore them if the originals are lost, damaged, or deleted.

Automatically back up my files
🔘 On

More options

Hot tip

You can create a system image (an exact copy of a drive) and also back up data files in the Libraries and other folders on your system. To select items to be backed up, click on **More options** in Step 3.

Don't forget

The **Recovery** option in **Update & security** has a **Reset this PC** option that can be used to reinstall Windows and select which files you want to keep.

System Restore

Windows 10 takes snapshots of the system files before any software updates are applied, or in any event once every seven days. You can also create a snapshot manually. The snapshots are known as Restore Points and are managed by System Restore.

1 From the Control Panel, open **System** under **System and Security** and select **System protection**

Hot tip

System Restore returns system files to an earlier point in time, allowing you to undo system changes without affecting your documents, email, and other data files.

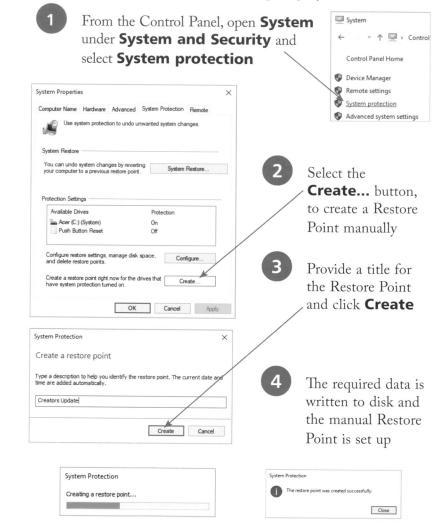

2 Select the **Create...** button, to create a Restore Point manually

3 Provide a title for the Restore Point and click **Create**

4 The required data is written to disk and the manual Restore Point is set up

Beware

System Restore is not intended for protecting personal data files. For these you should use Windows Backup (see page 227).

Using Restore Points

The installation of a new app or driver software may make Windows 10 behave unpredictably or have other unexpected results. Usually, uninstalling the app or rolling back the driver (see page 223) will correct the situation. If this does not fix the problem, use an automatic or manual Restore Point to reset your system to an earlier date when everything worked correctly.

1 Select **System protection** and click the **System Restore...** button

2 By default this will offer to undo the most recent change. This may fix the problem

System Restore

Restore system files and settings

System Restore can help fix problems that might be making your computer run slowly or stop responding.

System Restore does not affect any of your documents, pictures, or other personal data. Recently installed programs and drivers might be uninstalled.

< Back | Next > | Cancel

You can also run **System Restore from Safe Mode**, the troubleshooting option. Start up the computer and press **F8** repeatedly as your computer reboots, to display the boot menu, then select **Safe Mode**.

229

3 Otherwise, click a suitable item to use as the Restore Point

System Restore

Restore your computer to the state it was in before the selected event

Current time zone: GMT Daylight Time

Date and Time	Description	Type
4/25/2017 1:49:44 PM	Creators Update	Manual
4/21/2017 12:24:50 PM	Automatic Restore Point	System

Scan for affected programs

< Back | Next > | Cancel

If the selected Restore Point does not resolve the problem, you can try again, selecting another Restore Point.

4 Follow the prompts to restart the system using system files from the selected date and time

Security and Maintenance

The Security and Maintenance section in the Control Panel monitors security and delivers alerts for security features.

1 In the Control Panel, click on the **Security and Maintenance** link in **System and Security**

2 Select the **Change Security and Maintenance settings** link

Hot tip

In the Security and Maintenance settings you can also **Change User Account Control settings**, from a link at the side of the window.

3 Check the settings **On** or **Off** as required

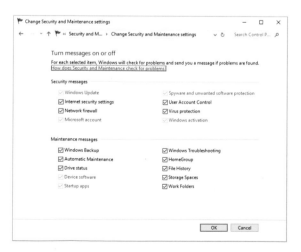

Windows Firewall

 1 Open the Control Panel, select the **System and Security** category and select **Windows Firewall**

Windows Firewall
Check firewall status
Allow an app through Windows Firewall

 2 Select **Turn Windows Firewall on or off** to customize settings for private (home and work) and public networks

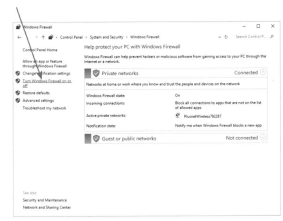

Hot tip

The Windows Firewall can be used to provide a level of protection against malicious software and viruses.

3 Select **Allow an app or feature through Windows Firewall**, to view the allowed apps

Allow an app or feature
through Windows Firewall

Don't forget

Firewall is on by default in Windows 10, but you can turn it off if you have another Firewall installed and active.

4 Click on the **Change settings** button to allow or restrict apps

Change settings

 5 Check apps **On** or **Off** to allow or remove them from the allowed list. Click on the **OK** button to apply the changes

Beware

Only add apps to the allowed list if you are advised to do so by a trusted advisor, or if you trust their origins.

Malware Protection

The Windows Defender app, which is pre-installed with Windows 10, can be used to give a certain amount of protection against viruses and malicious software. To use it:

Don't forget

Malware (malicious software) is designed to deliberately harm your computer. To protect your system, you need up-to-date antivirus and anti-spyware software. Windows Defender provides the latter, but you should install a separate antivirus app.

1 Select **Settings > Update & security > Windows Defender**

Windows Defender

2 Click on **Open Windows Defender Security Center**

Open Windows Defender Security Center

3 The Windows Defender window contains options for scanning your PC for viruses

NEW

The Windows Defender version in the Windows 10 Creators Update has been enhanced to provide more robust virus protection than earlier versions.

4 Select one of the scan options and click on the **Scan now** button

Scan options:

- ● Quick
- ○ Full
- ○ Custom

Scan now

5 The progress of the scan is indicated by the green bar. When the scan is completed, any issues will be listed with the suggested action to take

Your PC is being scanned

This might take some time, depending on the type of scan selected.

Cancel scan

Scan type: **Quick scan**

Index

Symbols

A

B

G

H

I

K

L

Q

R

S

T

U

V

W